ABCD

Attune
Build bounce
Correct with care
Develop disciplines relationally

If we were created for joy, and if every relational system in the world is modeled, ultimately, after the family, then who would not want to know how to raise joy-filled children who themselves then go on to be conduits of that joy in every institution they occupy? With *The 4 Habits of Raising Joy-Filled Kids*, Chris Coursey and Marcus Warner have given us a gem of a book that not only will change how you parent but also bring deep, lasting hope to all of your relational interactions. Read this book prepared to work. Read it prepared to be changed. But mostly, read it for the joy that is waiting for you as you do.

CURT THOMPSON, MD *author,* The Soul of Shame *and* Anatomy of the Soul

The journey from infancy to maturity is one that no child can make alone. Children need parents not merely to provide but to support and guide. But who will support and guide the parents? Marcus Warner and Chris Coursey have a keen understanding of the developmental needs of three-year-olds, thirteen-year-olds, and thirty-year-olds. Not only insightful but eminently practical, *The 4 Habits of Raising Joy-Filled Kids* is a primer every parent should read.

BILL ST. CYR, PHD *cofounder of Ambleside Schools International*

Chris Coursey and Marcus Warner approach parenting from a different perspective than any parenting book I have read. In *The 4 Habits of Raising Joy-Filled Kids*, they hold up a worthy goal: raising children who are motivated by relational joy instead of fear. My one critique of this book is that they didn't write this book twenty years ago when our kids were young. If you are a parent or if you know a parent, this book is a gold mine. I'm already counting how many copies I plan to give away.

MICHEL HENDRICKS *Director of Consulting at Life Model Works and coauthor of* The Other Half of Church

The *4 Habits of Raising Joy-Filled Kids*, Coursey and Warner provide needed resources to parents who want to build a relational home of joy and peace. This is what every parent who seeks counsel or coaching desires to learn. Every parent or soon to be parent wants this must-read book on how to raise resilient kids.

LORI A. MATEER, MA, LPC *Red Rocks Church University Classes Counselor/Trainer*

The 4 Habits of Raising Joy-Filled Kids is an excellent parenting resource! It is full of practical and helpful insights into building joy-filled kids while encouraging growth and maturity at every stage of development.

STEFANIE HINMAN, MS-ATR, BCCC *art therapist, counselor, coauthor of* Building Bounce, *author of* Building Bounce with Kids

Few jobs are more rewarding or difficult than that of parenting. Warner and Coursey, in their book *The 4 Habits of Raising Joy-Filled Kids*, offer solid help in navigating the challenging waters of parenthood. Their material is insightful, encouraging, and abundantly practical. You'll find that not only does their material equip you for becoming a better parent but a better person as well.

PAUL AND MARILYN HONTZ *parents of five adult married kids and fourteen "Grand Joys!"; author of* Listening for God *and* Shame Lifter

Where was this book when my kids were born? This is one of those books I will keep available for my coaching clients. Coursey and Warner have taken complex neuroscience and made it easy to understand and apply at every stage of your kids' development. Become the parent you want your kids to have. Read this book. Do the activities. Enjoy your family!

DAWN WHITESTONE *author of* Strategic Business Prayer *and founding partner of* WhiteStone Professionals

Jam-packed full of the best teaching on parenting, *The 4 Habits of Raising Joy-filled Kids* is a no-nonsense, practical book that very clearly and concisely explains the ABCDs of parenting. Like none other, this book is profound, yet simple and practical. It is my number-one resource for new and experienced parents alike. Sure wish this had been available twenty years ago. Thank you Chris and Marcus!

TONI M. DANIELS *Operations Director and Training Champion, LK10; author,* Back to Joy; *coauthor,* Joy Fueled

The 4 Habits of Raising Joy-Filled Kids by Marcus Warner and Chris Coursey is one of the best books I have read on parenting. They bring fresh ideas for emotional training in joy, maturity, and relating without fear. This book should be on every shelf—and read—where children are present. Practicing what Warner and Coursey propose will transform families, adults, and children of all ages.

BARBARA MOON *author of* Joy-Filled Relationships *and* Joy-Filled Parenting with Teens

Chris and Marcus are rock stars of clarity and practicality. They make the cutting-edge brain science of attachment understandable and useful. As a psychotherapist and a wounded healer, I have spent my life helping adults recover from early childhood attachment wounds. What a joy it is to read such clear guidance for parents longing to do a better job but not knowing what it looks like.

MARGARET M. WEBB, MA *Clinical Psychology, Wheaton College Graduate School; cofounder of Alive and Well, Inc., and Director of Immanuel Encounter Training*

The 4 Habits of Raising Joy-Filled Kids is refreshingly deep and simple at the same time—the acronyms make the power points simple to remember. ABCD, CAKE, VCR—we are already starting to rehearse them so they will be in our minds when we need them. We celebrate how Chris and Marcus are creating such wonderful and practical applications in our day through their recent books that embody the wise integration of sound theology and the latest neuroscience.

MICHAEL AND TERRI SULLIVANT *authors, speakers; Life Model Works; Radius Ministries; Terri Sullivant Coaching*

The *4 Habits of Raising Joy Filled Kids* taught us more ways to CREATE joy. Marcus and Chris provide tools to help you identify trouble spots in a constructive way with assessments and reflections. In addition, they provide practical ways to incorporate these joy-building techniques with practical "Habit Builder" exercises. Even while reading the book we started putting into practice some "Habit Builders" with our grandchild and witnessed results immediately by CREATING joy in a common low-joy situation!

JIM AND MICHELLE YEAGER *parents of adult children and grandparents to children; WOW Church*

This is a foundational book for parenting. I.e., you need to read this one first. Easy to read with exercises that can make joy a reality in your family—no matter how old your children are. Warning: this book can be challenging as it may reveal the holes in how you were raised or mistakes you have made with your kids, but it is also hopeful because it is so practical. It lays out exercises you can do to change the path of your parenting and your children forever.

STEVE MATEER

Chris Coursey and Marcus Warner masterfully show us what joy-filled families look like in clear, easy-to-digest chunks. I am so thrilled to have this new resource, *The 4 Habits of Raising Joy-Filled Kids*. Again, practicality, simplicity, and clarity make this book a gem for any parent. I will be giving away lots of copies.

LINDA KIMBROUGH

The 4 Habits of Raising Joy Filled-Kids is a concise and time-worthy bundle of help! If you've ever had parenting questions, you will now understand: the aim is to grow joy! I predict this easy six-chapter read will become a staple for families who will raise children filled with joy!

PAM BRYAN

Parenting is definitely the hardest job. We have these beautiful tiny little babes that grow into independent beings, with no handbook on how to parent. Well, great news. Chris and Marcus have packaged the tools needed for attunement and parenting in their book *The 4 Habits of Raising Joy-Filled Kids*. These are tools that I wish I had known when my children were still at home, but I still use them now to nurture healthy relationships with my children, and these tools help me to be the kind of "Nana" who is available and joyful.

ANNA HILL *Journey Church of God*

Bravo to Warner and Coursey for creating a stellar guide to parenting that integrates the wisdom of human development, attachment theory, brain science, and relational skills into a practical, approachable book. This is the best parenting book I have ever read because it addresses one of the heartaches of our world: that so few people understand what children and adults need—as well as what they need to master—to become joyful, resilient adults who are impacting our world for the good.

ELIZABETH MOLL STALCUP, PHD *executive director of Healing Center International and author of* Whispers in the Storm, Miracles, *and the* Facing Life's Losses *workbook*

I read this book as a father whose children have all left the "nest." In doing so, I was continually processing emotions that came to mind with the excellent illustrations by Chris Coursey and Marcus Warner. The most dominant emotion was deep gratitude that such a book has been written for parents. In speaking to the broad range of parents from those with infants all the way to those who have adult children, the authors have given our world and society a precious gift. All of us are starving for joy.

DANA BRYAN *Center City Chapel*

We pick up, read, and devour every book Chris and Marcus write together. The focus is on parenting, but it's applicable to all kinds of relationships. If there are any children you care about, I encourage you to buy this book and read it as it is not only for parents.

JOHN LOPPNOW *Relationship Coach and Therapist*

This is the most insightful parenting book we have ever read. It offers practical application that is grounded in wisdom and knowledge. The teachings made us painfully aware of our shortcomings yet simultaneously created a newfound hope for the parents we could become. If more parents applied these habits, we would empower generations to rise up and become mature adults filled with hope, joy, and the ability to bounce back from hardships.

CLINTON AND CHARITY MUNOZ *founders of Restored 2 More, Inc.*

The little-known secret gems found in this book will forever change how you view your role as a parent. The habits I discovered here have completely changed the way I parent. We found the habits could very practically be integrated into our daily lives. As I was reading, I was making a list of people I want to share this with!

JEREMY BERLIN, MS, LMFT *founder of* The Joy Couple

This is hands down one of the best parenting books I've ever read. It's simple, to the point, honest, and the practicality and the simplicity of the habits at the end of each chapter feel like small, doable action steps. It is also refreshing to hear from dads in this area, as the arena of expertise is generally flooded with moms. This is a book that I will be reading and rereading, along with purchasing multiple copies to hand out to friends and family.

LIEZA BATES *mother, author, and speaker*

We so wish we would have had this book at the beginning of our parenting adventure! Even though our boys are almost raised, *The 4 Habits of Raising Joy-Filled Kids* is such a valuable resource that will serve as your playbook no matter where you are on your parenting or grandparenting journey.

ANTHONY AND JEN HOPP

As a husband, father, grandparent, and family physician, I found this book to be not only about joy, but joy-filled in itself. The simple yet powerful paradigm for thinking about building joy at each stage of a child's life was easy to remember and allowed the fresh openness of each reader's story to shape the way they parent, yet with recognition of fruitful ways, which can be learned and applied, of developing your children into mature and joyful adults. These are joyful stories and a useful manual wrapped up in one small volume, a treasure for parents (and anyone who interacts with children) in any stage of life.

TIM DAVY

As a wife, mother, grandmother, and mentor, this little book is such a treasure not only for parents yearning to learn how to nurture and equip their children in a life-giving way, but also for the many of us who were missing these skills as children. The clear personal examples are very helpful in mentoring adults with maturity gaps.

SHELLEY DAVY

The 4 Habits of Raising Joy-Filled Kids shines a light on what is often a missing ingredient in family life: joyfully interacting in a way that builds emotional maturity and life skills. With explanation of what is needed at each stage of development and concrete description of how to build more joy and resilience, Chris Coursey and Marcus Warner explain how to grow as parents and how to help our children grow and thrive. We highly recommend it to anyone with children of any age.

JOHN AND MARY ELLEN SAUNDERS

The 4 Habits of
Raising *Joy-Filled* Kids

*A Simple Model for Developing
Your Child's Maturity—at Every Stage*

Marcus Warner *and* Chris M. Coursey

NORTHFIELD PUBLISHING
CHICAGO

Edited by Elizabeth Cody Newenhuyse
Interior and cover design: Erik M. Peterson
Cover illustration of hands copyright © 2018 by butenkow / iStock (1049701558). All rights reserved.
Chris Coursey photo: Charles Spoelstra

Library of Congress Cataloging-in-Publication Data
Names: Warner, Marcus, author. | Coursey, Chris, author.
Title: 4 habits of raising joy-filled kids : a simple model for developing your child's maturity-at every stage / Marcus Warner, Chris M. Coursey.
Other titles: Four habits of raising joy-filled kids
Description: Chicago : Northfield Publishing, [2021] | Includes bibliographical references. | Summary: "Joy-filled kids aren't always happy kids, but they do know how to work for and wait for what is truly satisfying in life. In The Four Habits of Raising Joy-Filled Kids, you will discover a toolbox full of skills that you can use with your children to help them grow in maturity and live with greater joy. The skills you learn will not only help you parent your children well, but they will also help you grow joy in your family"-- Provided by publisher.
Identifiers: LCCN 2020057844 (print) | LCCN 2020057845 (ebook) | ISBN 9780802421722 (paperback) | ISBN 9780802499240 (ebook)
Subjects: LCSH: Parenting. | Parent and child. | Joy in children.
Classification: LCC HQ755.8 .W374 2021 (print) | LCC HQ755.8 (ebook) | DDC 306.874--dc23
LC record available at https://lccn.loc.gov/2020057844
LC ebook record available at https://lccn.loc.gov/2020057845

We hope you enjoy this book from Northfield Publishing. Our goal is to provide high-quality, thought-provoking books and products that connect truth to your real needs and challenges. For more information on other books and products that will help you with all your important relationships, go to northfieldpublishing.com or write to:

Northfield Publishing
820 N. LaSalle Boulevard
Chicago, IL 60610

3 5 7 9 10 8 6 4 2

Printed in the United States of America

We dedicate this book to our kids with
thanks for the joy we have shared with them.
We love you lots!

CONTENTS

INTRODUCTION

A FEW YEARS AGO, I (Marcus) went to a local dealership to rent a car. I used to do this a couple times a month because my job required a lot of travel. But this time I had my wife and grown children with me. My wife and twenty-seven-year-old daughter were chatting like best friends. Suddenly and somewhat unexpectedly, my teenage son jumped on my back and surprised me with a bear hug. We both started laughing. I didn't really think anything of it until one of the workers looked up at us with wide eyes and said, "Will you adopt me? It's been a long time since I've seen a happy family."

My kids are now grown, but Chris and Jen have boys who are still in grade school. Recently, one of them asked Chris, "Why do you and Mommy smile at each other so much?" They must be doing something right to get a question like that!

No family is perfect, and even perfection can't guarantee results, because every person is unique. However, some families do live with a great deal more joy than others. So what is the secret? How does this work? Are they just lucky? Or . . . are there habits any family can develop that will give them the best chance to raise joy-filled kids?

You may be familiar with the opening line of Leo Tolstoy's classic novel *Anna Karenina.* It says, "Happy families are all alike. Every unhappy family is unhappy in its own way." He used this line to dive into the unhappiness of the families in his novel. However, we'd like to camp out on that first line a little longer. There is a lot of truth to the idea that happy families are all alike. This is because certain habits and practices characterize happy families regardless of ethnicity, culture, or religion. These same habits are noticeably missing in unhappy families—but, as we shall see, these practices can be learned.

At a large book expo in New York City, someone asked us, "What are your credentials for writing a book like this?" That is a good question. We both regularly provide training in brain science based relational skills. We also have spent decades helping people deal with past trauma and grow their emotional capacity. I (Chris) have worked with my wife to develop an extensive skills training program based on the latest brain science and attachment theory. Neither of us are marriage and family therapists. We don't run a clinic. However, we are both international speakers and authors who have helped a lot of families with the concepts and practices that have gone into this book.

Much of what is unique in this book comes from our relationship with Dr. E. James Wilder. He is a neuroscience specialist, and both of us have worked closely with him to develop practices for helping people understand attachment, grow maturity, and develop relational skills based on how the brain works. It was Dr. Wilder's brain research and the work of Dr. Allan Schore that created the "aha" moment for us about how important joy is to all of life.

According to these brain science experts, joy is relational happiness. Researchers have discovered there is an area of your brain that only grows in response to relational joy. We experience this joy when we see faces light up at seeing us, and we sense that *we* are the reason for the sparkle in their eyes.

We all need to know that we bring delight to others. Yet too many children feel unloved, unseen, and mistreated. Too many families overlook the vital importance of joy in building a strong family. This can change. It needs to change, and building the habits we describe in this book can serve as a catalyst for a joy revolution in your family.

Are you interested? If so, let's get started.

CHAPTER 1

Why Is Parenting So Hard?

YOU CAN'T BE A PARENT without feeling, at times, that for all the sense of reward and satisfaction in raising a child, it's also really, really hard. But why?

We think we've discovered a surprising reason why.

At the heart of this book is a unique idea: that families exist to grow joy. A clinical psychologist who has dealt with a lot of messy (and often scary) family dynamics through the years recently told me, "I've asked a lot of people what they thought the purpose of a family was, and none of them ever said that the purpose of a family was to grow joy." We want to change that. In fact, we hope this book launches a joy revolution, because we are convinced that transforming "low-joy" families into high-joy families can change the world.

What do "low-joy" families look like? When I (Chris) met my future wife, Jen, she could hardly get out of bed.

Jen grew up amid pervasive fear and depression. As a child, she struggled with suicidal thoughts and hopelessness. The depression was smothering her. It was hard for her to find hope, much less joy. Today, however, she and I train people in the skills and habits of joy-filled living.

This turnaround didn't happen overnight. It happened as Jen discovered specific skills she was missing. It was during this process that we met Dr. Jim Wilder and discovered the neuroscience of joy. Over time, we began intensive work focused on developing the missing skills in both of our lives. Eventually, with Dr. Wilder's guidance, we developed a training program that helps others grow these important skills.[1]

Jen's story offers hope at several levels.

- Low-joy beginnings don't mean low-joy futures are inevitable.
- People raised in low-joy families aren't doomed to raise low-joy kids themselves.
- Skills and habits can be developed that increase our own ability to live with joy.
- Those skills and habits can be passed on to our kids.

The primary purpose of this book is to introduce you to four habits for passing important skills on to your kids to equip them to live with joy in a low-joy world.

Raising joy-filled kids doesn't mean our kids are happy

all the time. That isn't even a desirable goal. Trying to keep our kids happy all the time just spoils them. Joy-filled kids see life as an adventure. They live with confidence that they can do hard things, develop curiosity and creativity, succeed at what is important, and recover from failure. They learn how to find the joy that is available to each of us every day of our lives and develop the skills to bounce back from hard experiences. In this sense, parenting is all about building the habits that grow our own capacity for joy and instilling those habits into our children. In the next chapter, we will explain the four habits of raising joy-filled kids, and in the chapters that follow, we will explain how to apply those habits as we parent our kids at the infant, child, and adult stages of life.

First, however, we want to take a look at why parenting is so hard, despite our best efforts to do it right.

WHY PARENTING IS SO HARD

Most parents have good intentions. Few of us bring children into this world with the express purpose of sucking the joy out of their lives and making them miserable. But it happens. It happened to some of us when we were kids. So why is parenting so hard, despite our best efforts to do it right? At the heart of many of our issues is the all-too-common reality that many of us are low-joy people from low-joy families. Here is a quick look at four characteristics of low-joy parenting.

1. Fear of failure. There is a major difference between fear-based parenting and joy-based parenting. Fear-based parents worry about messing up our kids. We worry what others will think of us. We can find ourselves trying to keep everyone happy, including our kids, only to discover that no one seems to be happy.

The fear of failure tends to make us angry, anxious, and avoidant. I (Marcus) can't tell you how many conversations I avoided with my kids until I got so angry that I finally said something I regretted. More than once I had to go apologize for snapping at my kids when the situation could have been resolved much earlier and with less distress if I hadn't been so avoidant.

Anxious parents are often clingy. They can't stand to see their children upset with them. Such parents often believe that the worst thing that can happen is for their kids to get angry at them. They then avoid conversations that might stir anger. They appease again and again, but it doesn't work. Their kids still end up angry. The point here is that avoidant parenting is fear-based parenting, and it doesn't produce joy-filled kids.

2. Lack of skills. As parents, we often feel overwhelmed. It can feel like we are piloting a plane we have no business flying because we were never properly trained how to read all the gauges and use all of the controls. When we lack parenting skills, we often go to one of two extremes.

We under-parent. When we under-parent, we like to

play with our kids, but we don't know what to do with the problems they face. It is not uncommon in families for one parent to be "the fun person," while the other, by default, becomes "the problem-solving person." It is easy to think that the fun person is the better parent, but that is often not true. Many times, the fun parent disappears when things get hard, leaving the other parent to handle the problems. It isn't that the other parent doesn't want to have fun, but they get abandoned to deal with the hard stuff so often, it becomes their role.

We over-parent. When we over-parent, we micromanage our children and become so focused on the problems we forget to have fun.

Chris and I don't point this out so that couples can fight over who is guilty of which extreme, but so that both can grow in their ability to work together.

Most of us picked up parental training by watching other people—especially our parents and grandparents. That is great if they were highly skilled and deeply loving people. However, if they lacked relational and emotional skills, chances are we don't have those skills either, because no one modeled them for us. In such settings, we become reactive parents. We have learned what we *don't* like and how we don't want to parent, but we do not develop important habits that help us raise mature children. A lack of healthy examples is the core reason for a lack of skills.

3. Unresolved pain. Unresolved pain can lead to a wide variety of parenting missteps.

Triggered parenting. Often, parents with unresolved pain get triggered and stop acting like adults. Triggered parents don't act like themselves—that is, they stop functioning like the caring, well-intentioned people they are and turn into someone others would hardly recognize. There were times I (Marcus) got triggered and felt angry as a parent. Most of the time, I remembered to excuse myself and calm down before I dealt with the issues, but now and then I would scold my child in the heat of the moment. It never produced good fruit. I always had to go back and ask for forgiveness and repair the relationship. I simply wasn't the same parent when I was triggered.

Distracted parenting. Many parents with unresolved pain are so focused on their own issues they don't give their kids the attention they need. Distracted parents are usually addicted to something—work, wine, TV, social media, novels, or darker attractions like porn and drugs. These addictions take priority over their children so that they are often out of touch with what is going on in their child's life. We have talked to many people who had to parent their parents when they were children. In one extreme case, a little girl we know lived with a mom who was regularly high and strung out on medications, which left the girl to not only get herself dressed, fed, and off to school on time, but to take care of her mom as well. It became the girl's job to make sure Mom was okay. The girl was only seven.

Reverse parenting. Reverse parenting happens when we expect our kids to take care of us, instead of the other way around. Many parents with unresolved pain use their kids and expect them to adapt *to their needs* rather than sacrificially caring for their children. Some parents live through their kids' achievements in sports, music, beauty pageants, and more.

4. Broken bonding patterns. If we were not raised with enough joy in our own family, we probably developed a broken bonding pattern that makes it difficult to form joyful bonds with our kids. Three of the most common fear-based bonding patterns are dismissive, distracted, and disorganized.[2] Those can be experienced on a spectrum (like one through ten). They can also overlap, but it is helpful to understand them individually first.

Dismissive bonding. A dismissive bonding style is like Teflon—nothing sticks. People with dismissive attachment tend to float from relationship to relationship and have trouble with commitment. They can be present with you but not really engaged.

Distracted bonding. A distracted bonding style is like Saran Wrap—such people tend to be clingy, and it can feel like no amount of bonding is ever enough. This attachment pattern develops when children's needs are not being met on their terms. Just like a child who doesn't get fed regularly begins to feel a desperation about the next meal, so a child who doesn't get connection at the times they need it will feel a similar desperation that creates this distracted bonding pattern.

Disorganized bonding. When the child wants to bond with Mom or Dad, but the parent is scary for some reason, the child will learn to be afraid to bond. They instinctively realize they are not safe and build a narrative around that feeling that says, "I want to be with Dad, but he can be mean. I'm not sure what to do." "I want to be close to Mom, but she gets really angry. I guess I'll stay away." It can also happen when the child sees that Mommy or Daddy is afraid. They think, "If they are afraid, maybe I should be afraid too." This can also work the other way around. Mom and Dad can have these feelings toward their kids. Disorganized attachment is the feeling that I want to be close to you, but I'm afraid of what will happen if I risk it.

THE CORE ISSUE: MATURITY

Low-joy homes produce low-maturity people. This is because joy and maturity are closely related. Maturity can be defined as the ability to handle hardship well because we have learned to remain relational, act like ourselves ("us" at our best), and return to joy.[3] Without maturity life becomes a constant pursuit of temporary pleasures, and relational joy becomes elusive. In order to grow joy-filled kids we need to guide our children to full maturity for the stage of life they are in. To accomplish this, we need to learn what maturity looks like at different stages of development.

One easy test of maturity is this: do our kids do things out of fear or out of joy? (We could ask ourselves the same question.) Immature people motivate themselves and others with fear. It takes continual practice in a variety of circumstances to learn how

> *When kids are motivated by joy, they feel like they can do anything.*

to motivate ourselves with joy. So it is with guiding our kids. When our kids are motivated by joy, they feel like they can do anything. They are adventurous, confident, willing to take risks. When our kids are motivated by fear, they don't like trying new things because they fear getting hurt or getting in trouble or being embarrassed or failing in a way they don't know how to handle.

Fear happens when we think we will get stuck in emotions that overwhelm us. This is why one child sees swimming as a joy and can't wait to leap off the high dive, and another child will avoid getting wet altogether. One knows that even if it hurts a little, they will recover and be okay. The other expects to be overwhelmed by their emotions and left to handle them by themselves. When I (Marcus) taught my daughter Stephanie to jump into the deep end of the pool for the first time, I stood right next to the side of the pool and made it super safe for her to explore the experience. She already knew how to swim. Her grandmother and mother had been playing with her in the water. My job was to help her overcome the natural fear of simply jumping into the deep end on her own. After jumping into my arms a few times and realizing she was okay, she started jumping in by herself as I watched. Before we were done, she was diving to the bottom of the pool and recovering coins I dropped there for her to find. Swimming and diving in the deep end of the pool stopped being scary, but we had to take it one step at a time. Notice I didn't stand on the side of the pool and shame her into jumping in. It was relational and age-appropriate, marked by little victories each step along the way.

Who doesn't want to raise good, loving, mature children? Every loving parent wants their kids to grow up to become good, successful people who flourish in their relationships. In the next chapter we want to offer you a simple model that provides guidance to what parents need to do with their children at each stage of development.

At the end of each chapter, we will provide you with questions and exercises to help you recognize patterns in your own parenting style and put into practice the four habits of raising joy-filled kids. We will start with two assessments.

FEAR ASSESSMENT

1. What do you fear most about parenting?
2. What robs you of your parenting joy most often?

Next steps:

- Connect with some friends and compare notes on how you answer these questions.
- Connect with some people from an older generation and see how they would answer these questions.

GAPS ASSESSMENT

1. Do you feel like there are gaps in the parenting "software" you downloaded from your family?
2. What parents do you know who have skills you wish you had?

Next steps:

- Schedule time to connect with these parents and ask them about how they handle certain aspects of parenting that are difficult for you.
- Share stories with these parents about some of your favorite parenting moments as well as "redemptive failures"—the times you messed up but learned something valuable and redemptive.

HABIT BUILDER #1—*Nonverbal joy*

1. Practice nonverbal joy as a couple.
2. Practice nonverbal joy with your kids.

The goal of these exercises is to make the other person smile without talking to them or tickling them or using props (like toys or tablets). You might try cuddling, holding hands, looking into each other's eyes, lighting up with excitement, and other such techniques.

HABIT BUILDER #2—*Add verbal joy*

Do the same two exercises as before but this time, add words of appreciation. What do you like about the other person? What about them makes you feel joy? Put that into words in addition to the nonverbal actions that you would normally use to connect.

Joy is best grown using your face, voice, body language, and words to convey "I am glad to be with you!" We want to find ways to convey joy that best match the age and stage of our children. For young children, you watch and wait for their attention, then light up with a big smile on your face. Watch to be sure your energy responses match their energy level, so you do not overwhelm them with too much stimulation. With older children, use nonverbal elements to start joy but include your words to share appreciation. It also helps to reminisce about moments of shared joy you have had together. Watch what happens!

CHAPTER 2

As Simple as ABCD

WHILE WE WERE DATING, I (Marcus) told Brenda that my greatest fear about getting married was becoming a parent. I was pretty sure I was going to mess up any kids we might have. She was very encouraging and told me I would make a great dad, but I knew the gaps I had experienced in my family, and I also knew I wasn't sure how to fix them. The thought of parenting brought joy to Brenda, but I was stuck in fear.

Now that we have been married for over thirty years and are empty nesters, I look back and realize I did do a lot of stuff wrong. I have learned a lot about parenting I wish I had known when we started. But even with the mistakes and challenges, it is a journey I wouldn't have missed for the world.

While Marcus and Brenda have grown kids, my wife, Jen, and I (Chris) are still early in the game of parenting.

We are putting these habits and concepts into practice in real time, and we can tell you they are making a big difference in our home.

In some ways, this is the book we both wish someone had given us when we were starting out—a "Parenting 101" book to explain the goals and strategies for raising mature children who are prepared to enter the adult world successfully. This book casts a vision for what it takes to guide a human from infancy to adult maturity. It identifies the important mile markers along the way and provides a practical guide for how to reach each mile marker. You aren't going to find another book quite like this. Our model is based on important breakthroughs in the understanding of attachment and human development. Building these habits will put you on the right track for raising joy-filled kids.

THE FOUR HABITS

We want to introduce you to four core habits and then provide you with practical steps to apply these habits at the infant, child, and adult stages of maturity development.

These four habits are based on the science of attachment theory. We have years of experience in training others in the relational skills taught here, and we have seen hundreds of couples and thousands of individuals experience real-life transformation as a result. You can think of these habits as the ABCDs of parenting. We will list them below and then explain them more fully in the rest of the chapter.

Attune. The first habit of effective parenting is attunement. Attunement is the art of reading your child's body language so you can recognize their emotional state and meet them there. Most of us know how to do this, but we have not made it a habit to connect with our children in their emotions before trying to correct behavior, fix problems, or give instructions. In fact, many of us expect our children to read *our* emotional state and adjust to us. We expect them to recognize when we are angry, distracted, or overwhelmed and know to leave us alone or treat us with greater sensitivity. Attunement is the job of the parent and the first habit of raising joy-filled kids.

Build bounce®.[1] Building "bounce" is about helping your kids learn the skills to recover from upsetting emotions. Our natural instinct is to protect our kids from any kind of pain. However, rather than Bubble Wrapping our kids, we are better off boosting their emotional immune system by helping them learn how to bounce back from hard things. One mom was understandably upset when she heard that a classmate had made fun of her daughter during recess. When she found out, the mom got angry and wanted to do something to make sure no one was ever mean to her daughter again. However, once she stopped to ponder the situation, she realized that this sort of thing was inevitable. Instead of pulling her daughter out of school or scolding the administrators, she taught her daughter how to stand up for herself and helped her recover the joy she had lost.

Our kids start as infants with no capacity to bounce back from hard things, but by the time they become adults, we want to train them in the skills they need to bounce back from all sorts of difficult emotions. The good news is that there are specific skills you can learn and pass on to your children to help with this. We will introduce a basic model in this chapter and expand on that in the chapters that follow.

Correct with care. Every parent has to correct their child. We want to help you learn how to correct behavior in a way that keeps the relationship bigger than the problem. As parents, we need to learn how to correct our children in ways that match their age and stage of development.

Develop disciplines relationally. If our kids are going to reach their full potential, we need to help them learn important life skills. At each stage of life, kids need to master certain disciplines. Each area of development provides a wonderful opportunity for us to bond with our kids and build some happy memories we can return to again and again.

Skills and habits don't just relate to tasks (like hitting a baseball, spelling words correctly, or riding a bike with no hands). They also involve dealing with emotions and relationships. The ABCD model takes this into consideration. A and B (Attuning and Building Bounce) relate primarily to emotions and relationships. C and D (Correcting with care and Developing disciplines relationally) focus more on tasks. These habits guide us in helping our kids develop the skills they need to live with wisdom.

RELATIONSHIPS	TASKS
A – Attunement	C – Correcting with care
B – Building bounce	D – Developing disciplines relationally

In the remainder of the book, we will explore how to grow each habit at each stage of life: infancy, childhood, and transitioning into adulthood. The habits remain the same at each stage of life, but the strategies change because you can't treat children like babies or adults like children and expect good outcomes. For now, let's take a closer look at the ABCD model for raising joy-filled kids.

Attuning

Attuning is recognizing the emotional state someone else is in and meeting them there. As parents, our job starts with attunement. We need to learn how to accurately read the emotional state of our children and meet them in their emotion in a way that lets them know we are not overwhelmed by what they are feeling and, in fact, we are happy to be with them. According to Dr. Stuart Brown, founder of the National Institute for Play, "When attunement occurs, both parents and child experience a joyful union."[2]

My (Marcus's) dad modeled this for me well. I remember watching him attune to my daughter when she was a baby. She was crying and no one seemed to be able to comfort her. My dad picked her up, looked her in the eyes, and mirrored the sadness in her face. He stuck out his bottom lip like he was pouting, and in a tender voice he said, "Oh, what a sad story! Life is so hard!" He was attuning to my daughter by meeting her in her emotional state. Then he began to help her bounce back from her upset emotions. He literally began to gently bounce her in his arms as he continued to make eye contact. His own face softened into a smile and her crying stopped. Soon, she was laughing and giggling. A few minutes later, she was quiet and content, and Daddy could take over. What I witnessed my father do was attune with my daughter's emotions in a nonverbal way. He let her know she was not alone. He began to soothe her with his touch, his voice, and his eyes. He didn't stop with attunement, either. He helped her build bounce. He helped her return to a place of joy and ultimately peace.

In their bestselling book *How We Love*, Milan and Kay Yerkovic observed that most of the couples who come to them for help with their marriages have no memories of being comforted by their parents. They don't remember anyone attuning with them or helping them bounce back from their distress.[3] Instead, far too many of us have memories of being abandoned with our emotions or worse, we were shamed or got punished for having emotions our parents didn't know how to handle. Raising joy-filled kids means we improve our ability to attune with our children's emotions and comfort them relationally. The more this happens, the more solid their emotional foundation will be.

We attune by "entering in" and sharing the emotional experience someone else is having. This helps people feel seen, heard, and understood. At each stage of life, we want to attune with our children in both verbal and nonverbal ways. Through our touch, voice tone, and eye contact, we want to communicate to our children they are in safe hands and it is okay to bring their big emotions to us. With age, we can use our words and help them use their words as we teach them how to comfort themselves. In this sense, attunement can be thought of as the relational bridge we build for our kids that allows them to move from distress to recovery. Without the bridge, they will likely get stuck in the emotional state they are in.[4]

When we don't take the time to attune, our kids feel unseen and unheard. Sending children to their room until they change their attitude or yelling at them to change the way they feel will do more harm than good. We attune with our kids by sending the message through both our body language and our words, "I'm with you here. You are not alone!" When our children feel alone with their upset emotions, their developing brains will find it nearly impossible to navigate their way back to joy.

We can tell when we are *not* attuning with our kids with a few simple tests.

- **Do we minimize our child's emotions?** We minimize our children's feelings when we say things like, "Get over it. Stop being a baby. It's not that big of a deal!" Minimizing our children's emotions declares that their emotions are not important, and it makes children feel like we don't care. Whenever we fail to validate their feelings, our kids will not feel seen, heard or understood. As a result, they will not trust what we have to say.

- **Do we abandon our child in distressing emotions?** We emotionally abandon our children when we say things like, "I can't handle it when you act like this. I need to get out of here!" Or, "Get out of here. I don't like you when you behave this way." When attunement is missing, children will feel alone in their own emotions, which makes the problem bigger.

- **Do we shame our child for having "big," intense emotions?** Do we welcome our children's feelings, or are they scary for us? If we feel threatened by their emotions, we often don't invite them to come to us for help. Instead, we can find ourselves shutting them down or shaming them. We may try to sidetrack them with "reasons" why they shouldn't be upset. Some parents shame their kids with expressions like "What is wrong with you?" "You don't see your friends acting like this, do you?" "You are such a crybaby!" Words like these create toxic shame. Labeling our children based on their upset emotions ("stupid," "baby," "whiner," "troublemaker") or comparing them with other people does great harm to their sense of identity. This approach creates distortions and reinforces the belief they are difficult and defective. In this sense, it actually trains children to stay immature.

- **Do we expect our child to make us feel better?** How often do we say things like "Can't you see I'm already upset?" "Why do you have to make everything worse?" "You don't want to see me angry, do you?" "Don't you care that I feel sad?" As adults, it is our job to attune to our kids and build a bridge for them to recover. It is not their job to build the bridge for us. Not only do many parents fail to attune to their kids and create a bridge back to safety, but they also expect their kids to create the bridge for them as parents. This can be thought of as "reverse parenting" or "upside down maturity."[5] This happens when we expect our kids to recognize where we are emotionally and adjust to us and our needs, rather than the other way around.

Building bounce

A second important habit for raising joy-filled kids is building bounce. We do this by helping our children grow their capacity for joy. You can think of joy as the air in a ball that lets it bounce. The more air, the better it bounces. If there is not enough air, the ball won't bounce back when you play with it. However, if it is full of air, the ball bounces back easily and naturally. Joy works the same way in our lives. Think about mornings when you wake up full of energy because something exciting is going to happen. Your joy gives you extra capacity to handle any hard stuff that may happen. By contrast, on those mornings when you wake up with very little joy, it can be hard to have the capacity to handle much of anything.

Just like muscles grow their capacity by working hard and then resting, joy grows by experiencing high-energy relational moments followed by satisfying, low-energy peaceful moments. Picture a baby cooing and giggling with Mommy and then falling asleep in her arms. Or a child wrestling with Daddy and then taking a break together to get some water.

Building bounce is about emotional regulation. This looks different at each of the three stages of development (infant, child, adult).

- **External regulation**. When our kids are infants, we do all of the regulating for them. They have no capacity to regulate their own emotions and quiet from them. If they are going to recover from their upset emotions, we are going to have to do all the work for them by attuning and comforting.

- **Co-regulation.** At the child stage, we *co-regulate* with our kids. We comfort them in ways that teach them the skills to begin comforting themselves. Every time we attune to their emotions and help them recover, we are empowering them to do this task for themselves later. Knowing that Mom and Dad are "on call" and will help them recover if they get stuck helps kids be more adventurous.
- **Self-regulation.** Once our children become adults, they should be well practiced in *self-regulation*—regulating their own emotions and ready to be a friend who can help others bounce back from their experiences with overwhelming feelings.

In some ways, building bounce is taking attunement to the next level. You will notice some overlap between these habits, because building bounce always starts with attunement, then adds the step of helping our children regulate their emotions.

When one of my (Chris's) kids was very young, the sound of the coffee grinder scared him. His face would show fear, and he would start to cry and want to hide behind furniture. We didn't understand this reaction, but knew we needed to help him learn how to build some bounce. One day, Jen sat with him while I ground the coffee. She got down on the floor and used her face, her calm voice, and (when he was ready) her touch to comfort him. After doing this intentionally a few times, he began to learn that feeling scared wasn't the end of the world because Mommy would be there. He also grew his capacity to the point that the sound wasn't frightening anymore.

Correcting with care

Parenting has a lot in common with coaching. Coaches want their players to reach their full potential and excel in a sport. Parents want their kids to be successful and excel in life and relationships. These goals require instilling discipline into our children (our next habit), and correcting mistakes they inevitably make in their attitudes and actions. Too many parents and coaches correct mistakes in toxic ways, and this can make it difficult, if not impossible, to approach life with joy.

Toxic correction is motivated by self-interest.

My (Marcus's) son has played on a variety of athletic teams since he was in elementary school, and he is now playing football in college. As parents, we have seen a lot of coaches. Some were excellent, and some were, well, toxic. The primary difference between a coach/parent who corrects with care and one who corrects in a toxic manner is not how tough they are, but *whose interest they have in mind.* Toxic correction is motivated by self-interest.

- I don't want to be embarrassed by you.
- I don't want you to think you can beat me.
- I don't want people to think of me negatively.
- I don't want this to be so hard.

Parents who think like this tend to correct in a manner that sucks the joy out of life. I remember one coach who used shame and anger to motivate his team. Even though he didn't directly shame my son, the culture created by this toxic motivation made my son so miserable, he started to despise a sport he normally loved. The same thing can happen with parents. If we correct our kids with toxic emotions, we quickly suck the joy out of life for them. Their goals start to involve keeping us out of their lives as much as possible. They may perform well enough to keep us from getting upset, but they can't wait to leave home and often find themselves trying to manage our immaturity rather than looking to us for the mentoring they need to handle the hardships of life with grace and maturity.

Correcting behavior looks different at each stage of development and under ever-changing circumstances. However, there are two principles we want to keep in mind in every situation.

1. We want to correct behavioral problems with our child's growth in mind (not our personal comfort or concern over our image).

2. We want to correct behavioral problems in a way that keeps our relationship with the child bigger than the problem. We do this by focusing our correction on *the child's behavior* and not their identity. We make a distinction: "Hitting your brother is mean" instead of "You're mean!"

Good parents correct their children because they love them and do not want to undermine their chances of success in life. When I had to correct my children as they were growing up, I often told them something like, "I love you, and I want you to be successful in life. I want you to be able to reach your goals and make lots of friends. Your behavior in this situation needs to be corrected because if you go down this path, it will not end well. The path of _____ will not take you where you want to go."

My goal was to help my children understand that my correction of their behavior was done with their interest in mind, out of a heart that deeply loved them. Correcting with care means we help our children feel seen and understood while we help them find a better path forward. There is never the threat of attack, nor is there a threat of losing the relationship.

For younger children especially, we keep the focus

on identity with positive statements such as, "We are kind people. We do not treat people unkindly; that is not like us." We help our children think through the consequences of their behavior with statements such as, "When we are kind toward others, people enjoy us and we make friends, but when we are unkind, people will tend to avoid us."

Jen and I (Chris) had an opportunity to correct with care when our son was six years old. We discovered our son was being mean toward another boy at a summer camp. That evening, we corrected our son with care by reminding him who he was and helping him think through how this behavior must have felt for the bullied child. The next day, our son apologized to the boy and made an effort to include him in all of the activities throughout the day. When the boy's mother showed up and heard about this, she wept because the boy was often bullied, but no one made the effort to apologize to him, let alone include him. It was very meaningful to have someone apologize and change their behavior to include her son. The smile on her son's face that day left an impression we will not soon forget.

Developing disciplines relationally

One of the goals that drove the way my wife, Brenda, and I (Marcus) parented our kids was pretty simple: We didn't want fear to keep them from experiencing life as an adventure. Toward this end, we tried to help our kids understand a basic life principle: the more skills you have, the more freedom you have, and skills require discipline. A common example of this would be playing the piano. If I lack skills, I won't have much freedom when I sit down at the keyboard. The only way I am going to gain the skills that give me the freedom to enjoy and master the piano is by developing discipline.

In order for our kids to experience life with freedom and see life as an adventure, we must teach skills and instill discipline into their lives. How we do this is the next challenge. My (Marcus's) father grew up during the Great Depression. His first car was a Model T. When he wanted to learn how to drive, his father told him he had to be able to take the car apart and put it back together first. His father was teaching him skills and disciplines. That was good. However, he didn't do it relationally. My dad was basically abandoned to figure it out for himself. He had the satisfaction of accomplishing something hard, but he has no lasting memories of time spent with his father working on the car together. It was a missed opportunity by his dad.

One of the skill sets my grandfather had that he didn't pass on was baseball. My grandfather was a star pitcher for the local team in the early 1900s. However, he didn't take the time to teach my dad the skills he had. As a result, my dad made sure he spent time with me and taught me all sorts of skills related to baseball. He taught my brother and me the mechanics of pitching and hitting and fielding. We practiced together for hours, and he often invented new training techniques to help us learn. In other areas, however, my dad's attitude tended to mirror what he had learned from his father. More than once I heard him say, "If you want to learn how to do _____, go to the library, check out some books, and figure it out." That was okay, but not what I wanted. I wanted the relational connection that came with the investment of time. I have had the same issue with my kids. In some areas, I spent a lot of relational time passing on skills, in others, I was absent and missed the opportunity.

It was common in my dad's generation for parents to have a "sink or swim" approach to teaching life skills. This instilled independence, but attunement was lacking. The boomer generation I (Marcus) grew up in went to the opposite extreme. We were so focused on attuning to emotions, we often didn't teach independence. The idea behind developing disciplines relationally is to combine the best of both of these approaches.

When we help our kids develop disciplines relationally, we are passing on much more than just the skill itself. We help our children learn patience and perseverance. We teach them how to navigate failure and celebrate success. Developing disciplines relationally teaches children they are not alone in hard times. The loving

We need to be honest with ourselves and with our children about the mistakes we make, as well as the holes in our own development.

presence of a parent allows us to share our emotional capacity with them. They can handle more when they feel "We are in this together!" as opposed to "I am in this by myself."

OUR BIGGEST PARENTING OBSTACLE

The biggest obstacle to successful parenting is our own immaturity. Maturity is about developing the strength and skills to persevere and recover from hardship. As parents, we inevitably discover holes in our maturity as we try to raise our kids. We don't attune. We fail to build bounce. We correct in unhelpful, even toxic ways. We instill disciplines in toxic ways, or we simply do not train our kids with important skills because we never learned them ourselves. However, parenting is not a job for perfect people. It is a job for honest people. We need to be honest with ourselves and with our children about the mistakes we make, as well as the holes in our own development. The goal isn't to justify ourselves, but to be honest that we are all incomplete people. We also want to model what it looks like to keep growing throughout life. If we get good at repairing problems we create with our children, it helps take some of the pressure off.

If your parents did not attune with you, this ability will probably not come naturally to you when you try to attune with your children. Learning to attune requires practice. We need to practice reading our children's emotions and validating them. We know we have succeeded when the child feels understood and wants to connect. In order to build this habit, you will need to be really intentional about practicing and growing new skills. The good news is this. Many people who grew up in terrible families end up becoming really great parents. This is because they often work extra hard at developing the skills they missed, whereas those who grew up in "pretty good" families are content being "pretty good" parents. As a result, they do not feel as motivated to achieve excellence in their parenting.

In this chapter, we learned a simple model for raising joy-filled kids—ABCD. In the chapters ahead, we will explore three core stages of maturity development—infant, child, and adult—and explain how the four habits of this model can be applied at each stage. We will review some of the essential skills that need to be developed at each life stage and offer practical guidance on how the four habits mentioned in this chapter can be applied.

4 HABITS ASSESSMENT/REFLECTION

1. When you consider attunement, building bounce, correcting with care, and developing disciplines

relationally, what areas do you feel you do well? What areas need some work?

2. What parenting lessons or wisdom did you learn from your parents that were good and helpful? What would you like to do differently—or wish you had done differently—than your parents did?

3. When you look back on parenting your child/children, what are the lessons and wisdom you will be glad you instilled in your child/children?

HABIT BUILDER #3—*Share joy creatively*

At the end of the day, we want our children to feel loved and valued by us. How do you help your children feel loved? Time and attention are some of the best gifts you can give them.

1. Make it a point to spend an evening or afternoon doing something they enjoy. Invite your children to pick what activity they want to do.

2. Establish a clear expectation before you begin that at some point, time will be spent talking about highlights from your day or your week. The point is to spend time talking about good stuff. This may happen on the way to where you are going or perhaps over food when you are all done. Have fun and amplify some joy.

HABIT BUILDER #4—*Redemptive parenting*

Good parents are not the people who parent perfectly without ever making mistakes. Good parents are those who are quick to apologize when mistakes are made. They work hard to repair the relationship when ruptures happen. They try to fill in gaps when they discover specific holes in their own maturity. They work at developing skills they missed so they have more to pass on. These actions help children feel seen, understood, and cared for.

Here are steps to take when we make mistakes as parents.

1. With infants we try to restore a sense of safety and connection.
2. With children we use words to let them know we did not act like the parent we want to be.
3. With adult children it can help to write a letter to or have a conversation where you take ownership over the mistakes you made. Let them know the kind of parent you want to be. Highlight some of the qualities you enjoy about them. Share reasons you are proud of your child.

(Note: This is not the time to justify or explain away your mistakes. Simply acknowledge, take ownership over, and apologize for the pain you caused. Otherwise, you risk making excuses for your mistakes or minimizing the impact of your mistake, which erodes trust.)

CHAPTER 3

Raising Joy-Filled Infants

WHEN MY WIFE, BRENDA, gave birth to our first child, it wasn't an ideal experience. Her body struggled with the pregnancy. A few weeks before the due date, she went in for an appointment and was about to be sent home when she reminded the doctor that her numbers had been elevated. The doctor took a second look and ordered that she be induced immediately. Our visit went from a checkup to an emergency.

The story gets worse from there. After my wife dealt with eight hours of induced labor pains, the doctor realized that the baby was breech and that she needed a C-section. They rushed her into the operating room while I changed into scrubs to be with her. I got locked out of the operating room. They started the procedure before her anesthesia kicked in. When I finally got into the room, she was in pain and gripped my hand so tightly her fingernails drew blood. In the end, however, we were presented with a perfectly adorable little girl. In an instant, we couldn't imagine life without her.

From the very beginning, parenting is about sacrifice. Mothers go through a great deal of sacrifice to bring their babies into the world. As parents, we sacrifice our own comfort and pleasure in order to attune to our baby's needs. We want to make sure they are protected, loved, and nurtured. We are counting on help from those who have gone before to guide us on how to care for our little ones. That is what this chapter is about.

FUN FACTS ABOUT BABIES

To help us get started it might be helpful to know a few facts about babies.

1. Babies are born with a deep need to attach. The way the human brain works, the deepest craving a baby has is for *attachment*. Joy is the one thing a baby will actively seek out.[1]

2. Babies initially experience attachment through smell, touch, taste, temperature regulation, and hearing before sight. Long before baby looks up at you with recognition and lights up with delight, the little one is already bonding through these other senses.[2]

3. Babies are not born with the capacity to regulate emotions on their own. We have to recognize what

they need and respond accordingly with focused attention and consistency so they can predict good things follow whenever they have a need. We always comfort them during times of distress. We don't leave them to "cry it out" or they become insecure— never knowing when their needs will be met and when they will be ignored.

4. By comforting our infants again and again, their brains begin to form pathways that allow them to return to joy from upsetting emotions more quickly. Eventually, they begin to learn how to quiet on their own. Quieting from upset is one of the most important skills a baby can learn and is the number one predictor of stable emotional health.[3]

5. Babies are not born with a single identity. The part of the brain that thinks of itself as "me" is not fully formed at birth.[4] As a result, infants act like completely different people, depending on the emotion they feel.[5]

This is not always obvious while they are infants, but it shows up clearly in the child stage. When babies express fear or anger or sadness or other big emotions, it is our job to read them correctly, meet them in their emotions and help them recover. If we don't help them in this way, their brains will not learn how to stay themselves during upset. If we didn't get help with these skills, even as parents we can turn into someone different when we are upset. Here is a quick self-assessment for the parent.

- Do people walk on eggshells when I get angry? Do others fear my anger and try to keep me happy? If so, I haven't learned how to stay myself when I get angry.
- Do I receive correction well? Or do others fear correcting me and telling me when I am wrong? If so, I haven't learned how to stay myself when I feel shame.
- Can fear make me switch from relational and connected to shut down and distant in the same conversation? If so, I have not learned how to stay myself when I am afraid.

6. One of the key tasks of parenting at the infant stage is helping babies develop the capacity to act like themselves regardless of which emotion they feel. We do this primarily by attuning to their needs and comforting them over and over again. By the time the infant reaches childhood they should have seen us bounce back from upset emotions hundreds of times and they should have received our help in bouncing back from difficult emotions hundreds of times. The more they see us recover and get help with their own emotions, the more stable their identity will be as they enter childhood. This is why

it doesn't work to say, "Do as I say, not as I do." Our kids see what we do and follow our example. This is why we often pick up unwanted habits from our parents we didn't even know we had learned.

7. Babies have an underdeveloped capacity for joy when they are born. However, as we practice joy workouts on a regular basis (more to come on that), the joy center in their brain can grow until joy becomes the default setting in the brain. Based on these important points, we want to maximize joy and look at what it means to practice the ABCDs of raising joy-filled kids when our kids are infants.

ATTUNEMENT WITH INFANTS

Parents attune with their infants when they respond to their baby's emotions—whether they are upset or joyful—with focused attention that shares the feelings with the baby. When the feelings are negative, this "sharing" shows infants how to recover. We mirror their upset emotions on our faces and help them return to joy. When the feeling is joy, parent and baby share the joy together, which makes both of them feel connected.

If our little one is fussy or upset, we learn to "read" their emotional state. We come to their aid and attune by using our face, voice tone, and touch to say, "You are not alone; I am with you." While we are doing this, we are also problem-solving. We want to know why they are upset. Are they hungry? Is something pinching them? Do they need a new diaper? When we correctly identify the problem and meet the need *while remaining relationally engaged*, baby learns getting upset is not the end of the world. Upset leads to comfort and connection.[6]

There is a path back to joy from their upset emotions. When I (Chris) first had to change a diaper, I removed it too soon and exposed a "cannon" that blew a mess everywhere. I remember his face looking at mine as if to ask, "Is this too much for you? Are we going to get through this?" I realized it wasn't enough for me just to get the job done. I had to let my son know I was still happy to be with him even though this was truly disgusting. I wrinkled my nose as if to say, "Yuck! This is nasty!" but then I smiled at him and let him know with my voice tone that I was still happy to be with him and that everything was going to be okay.

The combination of synchronizing with baby's emotions and meeting their needs creates security as well as stability. It instills a foundation of joy for life. Skills like these come naturally for some of us because we had them modeled so much in our families. But for others, we need a road map. If you have to learn this skill from scratch, it can be helpful to understand how it works step by step.

With infants, we figure out what the needs are and we try to meet the needs quickly and safely. As we will explore in chapter 4, children learn to use words for what they need. In this way, children learn to ask for what they need and how well this goes depends on how well we meet needs during the infant stage of life. At the infant stage, attuning is the response to baby's ever-changing needs. We are responding to what we see baby doing and needing. We are not expecting baby to recognize what

Infants need to know they are not alone and someone is always ready to meet their needs.

we need or want. Our job is to care for baby's needs.

One of the practical principles that grows out of this is that you never leave a baby to "cry it out," as if that is going to teach them a lesson. We have heard parents say, "Just let them cry, or they'll think they can have whatever they want anytime they want it just by throwing a fit." This is actually not true and has more to do with the parent's fear than it does the baby's needs. Infants need to know they are not alone and someone is always ready to meet their needs. We are not going to spoil them by taking care of their needs.

As children grow older, this is a different story. When they are between the ages of four and twelve, they start to learn to tame their cravings, and in this stage of life, they can wait for and work for what they want. We'll get to that in the next chapter. However, an infant is incapable of "learning" such a lesson. The infant will only learn insecurity. If we let them cry it out now, baby will never know when their needs will get met and when they won't. This creates distress for baby, and they lose confidence that their cries will be answered and their needs met. They are not sure when they will be ignored and when they will be comforted. Such inconsistency creates anxiety and instability. The infant can only experience this type of neglect as abandonment as the brain's survival center kicks into high gear with fear while the attachment circuits "feel" all alone. We do not want infants feeling alone in their distress.

Before the brain science revolution in the '90s there was a lot of debate about this topic. Many people remember their parents saying, "You gotta let him cry it out or he'll never learn!" A woman of our acquaintance recalled raising her daughter in the '80s: "Both my mother and mother-in-law were old school, 'let her cry.' So were some of the leading experts of the time, although a few mavericks were starting to question that idea, and brain science later confirmed what she as a mom knew by instinct: "When my baby cries, I go help." Understanding the brain has changed this let-them-cry mindset. We now know that letting an infant cry it out creates an insecure attachment, which leads to fear rather than joy.

BUILDING BOUNCE WITH INFANTS

As we've seen, building bounce is about resilience, the ability to bounce back from upset emotions. Infants have no resilience when they are born. They must borrow ours to begin with. There are two important practices that can help babies develop their emotional resilience: joy workouts and recovery workouts.

A joy workout is about recognizing that our baby wants to grow joy and engaging with them. This process combines two important elements: (1) smiling playfulness followed by (2) quiet and rest. If you are familiar with weightlifting, you probably know that body builders don't grow muscle while they are lifting weights. The workout itself is actually breaking down their muscles. The growth happens during the period of rest between workouts as the muscles repair the damage that was done. In a similar way, a baby grows its capacity for joy by both the smiling, playful part of the engagement and the rest in between. The brain's joy center needs the rest as much as it needs the smiles if it is to grow big and strong.

By nine months of age, babies will spend up to eight hours seeking joy smiles per day.

By nine months of age, babies will spend up to eight hours seeking joy smiles per day.[7] That's a lot. Probably more than most of us can do. This is one of the reasons babies need lots of people in their life who are happy to see them. Joy is euphoric for baby. Dr. Allan Schore teaches that smiles release natural opioids in baby's brain, and smiles trigger processes that help brain neurons grow.

Smiles are not optional; baby needs joyful smiles in order to grow!

Early in their development, infants learn to track eyes, and infants look to the eyes to find joy.[8] Infants are actively looking for eyes that say, "You are delightful! You make me happy! I love you!" When our faces light up with joy and baby notices our delight in them, their feelings of joy create a physical reaction inside that makes them smile and giggle and squirm with glee. Brain science expert Dr. Allan Schore writes about baby and mother sharing joyful glances, "Thus, how often and in what contexts the mother and infant *spontaneously* look (and not look) directly at each other is of key importance to an infant's development and the emotional health of the dyadic relationship."[9]

You may notice that babies can suddenly shut down and look away in the middle of all of this joy. That is not a problem. This means baby's brain has reached its capacity for joy. This next statement is really important. You need to allow baby to rest and recover while you stay attentive for baby to return her gaze, which is the invitation for more joy.

Too many parents think, "Joy is good. More joy must be better," and they inadvertently push baby to keep engaging playfully after the infant has had enough and looked away for a breather. Repeatedly ignoring a baby's need for a break will be experienced as a type of attachment trauma by the infant.[10] In a sense, they are establishing a boundary, only to have someone cross it. It creates a feeling of overwhelm and distress because someone is intruding on their need for recovery.

A major part of attuning is making sure we build joy and return to quiet on the infant's schedule. This is called *synchronizing*. We need to synchronize with our baby's emotions. When they are ready for joy, we jump in and share joy with them. When they are ready for rest and quiet, we need to let them have a breather and recover. Joyful glances build joy, and relational disconnects bring rest. The baby sets the schedule.

Here are a few joy workout options. Remember, every joy workout should end with rest and peace.

- Eye-smiles—Make eye contact with the baby and share smiles until the baby looks away, then begin again when the baby looks back at you.
- Peekaboo—This fun practice rewards the baby's natural desire to look for eyes that sparkle with delight at them.
- Joyful sounds—Make funny, happy sounds (and facial expressions) so baby hears the joy in your voice. "Motherese" is a type of exaggerated baby talk that happens when an adult speaks to a young child, which helps children develop language skills faster.[11] The role of "motherese" by a caregiver plays

a crucial role for the developing brain learning to recognize the meaning and intent of voice tones later in life.[12] Research also shows that the kind and quality of mother's voice tone can create feelings of safety and help children recover from upset emotions and return to feeling safe.[13]

- Snuggling—Cuddling and cradling your little one creates a secure bond and increases the bonding hormone oxytocin, which personalizes our joy and generates feelings of safety, trust, and generosity. Babies learn to seek out the smell and feel of their caregiver. Affectionate touch is essential for the development of the emotional areas of the brain.[14]

- Play—Playful interaction should be fun and exciting, but not too scary. One way to keep play manageable and within the "fun range" is to stay alert to signals that the infant has had enough stimulation and needs a breather. It is important to pause so baby can rest and recharge at the right times. Play provides the opportunity to build joy, deepen the bond, and gain important relational skills.[15]

Recovery workouts are about helping our little ones bounce back from overwhelming emotions. A recovery workout begins when our infant is feeling distress. At this point, two specific steps are needed. First, their emotions need to be validated. This means we attune to them in their big emotion and let them know through our eyes, facial expressions, and voice tone that we understand what they are feeling. During the toddler years, we can begin using words to let them know we understand what the emotion is and just how big it is for them. If my son falls and scrapes his knee, my eyes will get big and share his sense of fear. This lets him know I see and understand what he is feeling. Then I can help him fix the problem. I may point to his knee, put a pout on my face, and say, "Oh, you have a boo-boo." Once he feels like I have met him in his emotion we can move on to cleaning the wound, putting on a bandage, and making sure he feels "all better."

Validation doesn't mean we think children "should" feel the way they do; it means we recognize this is how they feel, and we understand just how big the emotion is. For example, my son may get really angry that his brother isn't sharing a toy. I may not think he should be angry, but I'm not going to get anywhere until I take the time to meet him in that anger and move forward.

The second step (after validation) is comfort. We need to do something to resolve their problem. We may need to change a diaper, or get some food, or give a hug, or stay present and engaged while they recover. We can tell when they have recovered, and the workout is over because their face relaxes, and their breathing will return to normal. They appear to feel calm and peaceful again.

The recovery workout process can be remembered with the letters VCR—*Validate, Comfort, Recover.*[16] This process needs to be done with every upsetting emotion our children face. There are six core negative emotions that need their own pathway back to joy.[17]

1. Shame: the feeling I am not bringing you joy and you are not glad to be with me.
2. Sadness: the feeling that I lost some of my life.
3. Anger: the feeling I need to protect myself and make something stop.
4. Fear: the feeling I want to get away.
5. Disgust: the feeling something is not lifegiving.
6. Despair: the feeling that I lack the time and resources for something vital.

We don't list these to overwhelm you, but to make it clear that each of these emotions requires validation and comfort repeatedly in order for the brain to develop a pathway from distress back to a state of calm, safe, and joyful connection.[18]

CORRECTING INFANTS WITH CARE

When it comes to correcting infants (birth to age three or four), there is one very important fact that needs to be understood. Until their brains develop more fully, infants don't understand negative commands. If I say, "Don't hit your sister!" My infant hears, "Blah, blah, blah, hit your sister!" If I say, "Don't touch that!" the baby hears, "blah, blah, blah, touch that." Their brains aren't able to process the negative part of the command. They simply haven't developed this capacity at their young age. This has some significant implications.

- We need to be careful not to label our kids as "rebellious" or "strong-willed" when they enter the "terrible twos." There is a lot going on there and we will discuss it more down below, but often the problem is not with our kids; it is with our communication.
- We need to learn to state what we want in positive terms. We need to speak the toddler's language as if we are having a cross-cultural experience. Friend and attachment expert Jim Wilder writes:

> All important commands given to children under five should be positive. If you have trouble making positive commands out of negative ones it will help you understand the impossibility this poses for the two-year-old mind. Negative commands must be translated by the parent's brain into useful instructions the child can follow. For instance:
>
>> "Don't hit your sister!" becomes "Play nicely with your sister."
>> "Don't touch it!" becomes "Keep your hands down and look!"
>> "Don't leave the yard!" becomes "Stay in the yard!"[19]

When little ones do respond to negative commands, it is not the words they are responding to; it is their ability to "read" your tone of voice. They learn to recognize when your voice is giving them the green light to go ahead with what they are doing, or the red light that says, "Stop!"

When it comes to "the terrible twos," we have some good news. The twos don't have to be terrible. It can help to understand what is going on inside our toddlers at this age. Around sixteen months after birth, the limbic system matures enough to become more active. This detail may not mean anything to most of us, but once activated, the limbic system allows anger to become rage and fear to become terror. The amplifier in the brain is turned on! This is why your darling toddler can have gigantic reactions, and eventually say horrible things like, "I hate you!" or "I wish my brother was dead!" They are trying to put words to the fact that really intense emotions are going on inside, and they don't know what to do with them. If we deal with such situations as reasons for punishment, we will just make the problem bigger. Two-year-olds who are having such tantrums don't need to be controlled and stopped so much as they need someone to show them how to manage their feelings and return to joy.

To quote Dr. Wilder again: "Parents who make control the number one issue at this age will not produce courageous children. Returning to joy is the number one priority; learning to obey is number two."[20] This means we need to help them bounce back from their emotions before we try to correct their behavior. Parents who remember to keep these priorities straight often have far more joy with their two-year-olds than those who don't.

HEALTHY SHAME

There is a difference between healthy and toxic shame.[21] Some people think all shame is bad because they are only familiar with toxic shame. Toxic shame has two elements. (1) A person feels alone in their shame—like no one is happy to be with them. As long as there is connection and attunement, shame is not a big deal from the brain's perspective. It is more like a speed bump than a pothole. When a person feels alone in their shame it becomes toxic. (2) A person's identity is attacked, not just their behavior. Toxic shame attacks a person's identity or character—"You're bad, you're stupid, you never get things right"—that's toxic shame.

> *If we never feel shame, we will never change the behaviors that annoy others.*

Shame can be healthy. In fact, it is indispensable for correcting and maturing. If we never feel shame, we will never change the behaviors that annoy others. Shame is only healthy when attachment is maintained. When behavior is corrected, that correction may make someone feel bad, and it is not always wrong to make someone feel bad. Sometimes our kids need to know that what they have done has disappointed us. If my son pulls down his pants and relieves himself in a potted plant in the middle of the mall, he's going to get a reaction. At that point, I am not going to be happy with him or his behavior. But I still love him. The relationship is not threatened. The behavior is what needs changing. I will correct him by saying something like, "We don't do that, buddy." The correction may cause him temporary shame, but if I stay relational through the correction and we reestablish that I am happy to be with him, the shame doesn't need to be toxic. Events like this update the child's brain so they learn which behaviors are acceptable to others and which ones aren't.

It is important for children to learn how to feel shame and recover, or they will not form a healthy identity that embraces correction. People who don't learn to process shame and recover are far more likely to become narcissists later in life.[22] Part of correcting with care involves learning to give a healthy shame message and avoid toxic shame.

A healthy shame message has the following elements:

- It affirms a positive identity for the child.
- It communicates that there is a problem that needs to be corrected.
- It preserves the relationship and makes sure that the correction ends with relational connection.
- It provides opportunities for growth.

Toxic shame looks completely different.

- It attacks the child's character and identity.
- It communicates that the child is the problem.
- It makes relationship conditional on good behavior.
- It abandons the child in their feelings of shame, which hinders growth.

Healthy shame provides an opportunity to learn something valuable and change our behavior. Let's say an infant makes a mess in their diaper and decides to dig it out and show Mom and Dad what they've found. The parent's wrinkled up nose displays disgust and sends a healthy shame message. Infants can tell by the parent's face something about this was not good. At this point, the parent needs to provide a path back to relationship by changing their disgust back to an expression that says, "I'm glad to be with you," then help them understand that it is not like us to share the mess in our diapers.

Part of what makes shame toxic is abandoning our children in their shame. If your child runs across a busy intersection, you may need to react quickly to stop them, then follow up with, "I want you around for a long time, so listen when I tell you to stay on the sidewalk." You might give them a hug at this point. That is a healthy shame message with a path back to relationship. Toxic shame would say, "You are so stupid! What were you thinking?" then abandon them to recover on their own.

As we've mentioned, Chris and Jen have two boys, Matthew and Andrew. One day one of them took his brother's new toy and the other little guy started crying. It was clear by the look of disapproval on Chris's and Jen's faces this behavior was unacceptable. They responded with a look of displeasure and said, "We are kind to brother. Give him his toy back and we will find you a toy you like." Once their son saw the facial expressions and heard Mom's and Dad's voice tones, he understood this behavior was not acceptable. At this point he was feeling shame. He returned the toy to his brother. To help him recover from his shame, Chris's and Jen's faces lit up with enthusiasm and they clapped their hands, saying, "Good job, son! You are a kind boy." The healthy shame message provided an opportunity for their son to correct his behavior while Chris and Jen stayed relationally connected with him and affirmed the positive identity of their son.

DEVELOPING DISCIPLINES RELATIONALLY WITH INFANTS

During the first half of infancy, babies don't really need to learn disciplines. They just need to be taken care of. As they enter the toddler years, we begin to teach them to use their words, how to go potty, how to drink from a cup. These are big opportunities for relational bonding. We are with them—and happy to be with them—through success and failure. Positive reinforcement is key during this time. Infants like to see a big joyful reaction when they do something well, and will often repeat the actions that generate the joyful response in a parent's face.

Frustration becomes an opportunity to help your child return to joy. It is a good time for a recovery workout. The VCR process is important when our kids get upset as they try to learn new skills. Upset emotions are always a chance to develop emotional regulation skills.

Toddlers often need to be taught not to do things. This is particularly challenging when you can't use negative commands to instruct them. This is where the nonverbals really help. Let's say my toddler bites a friend who came over to play. My child should see immediately that this didn't bring joy to anyone. The other child may be crying, and my face and voice tone should reflect that I am not happy. This alerts their brain that something is wrong. The nonverbal cues tell a story to the toddler. Since they don't understand negative commands, the nonverbals are especially important. We may explain, "Biting hurts people. We need to be kind. We need to use our words not our teeth." We then walk them through the right way to do something. Sometimes it is helpful to reenact the event and say, "Let's try that again," then coach them through the right way to handle their upset emotions. Before we move on, we want to help everyone bounce back from their upset emotions and recover.

Sometimes it is not the kids who get angry or frustrated.

We are the ones who fail. We blow it and handle situations the wrong way. Sometimes we overreact with our kids, and sometimes we do things in front of them that are inappropriate. Maybe we yell at someone while we are driving and get so angry that we scare our child. When we fail, we need to work on our own ability to bounce back from our big emotions. Let's say I yelled in anger at someone as my child watched. I may need to help them interpret that experience. My goal is not to justify myself. My goal is to be honest and say something like "I got really frustrated and didn't act like myself for a moment. I didn't mean to scare you. I am sorry for this. Daddy will be okay, and you do not need to fix this problem."

THE PATH AHEAD

Growing joyful infants is a valuable journey that requires patience, much practice with joy and rest, and lots of consistency and predictability when it comes to meeting baby's needs. Babies are "bonding machines" born to attach and at the mercy of parents and caregivers to meet their needs. Parents, caregivers, and family members help baby grow joy when they stay attentive to baby's ever-changing needs. This stage can be greatly demanding on any parent's capacity. Baby's needs are big, immediate, and constant. Parents need the support of a community to stay joyfully tuned in to their own needs as they sacrificially care for children. This stage is a good time for parents to ask for help and find peers who can encourage and coach them along.

HABIT BUILDER #5—*Create a calm environment*

1. Consider the ways you use your face, voice, body language, and words when you are with your baby and family members. Baby will bond with whatever is in the environment, and everything from sights to sounds and smells will either become familiar and comforting or scary and overwhelming. The point of these questions is to help us become more aware of the type of environment we are creating for our babies. We want to maximize the sights, sounds, and smells that create peace rather than upset.

   a. What expression do you wear on your face when you interact with your family members? (Look in a mirror if you have to!) Many parents think they smile a lot more than they really do. Do our little ones see our faces as checked out, anxious, angry, or is our normal expression one of calm and joy?

   b. In your house, what sounds is your baby bonding with? Is there a lot of arguing? Is there loud, angry music in the background, or is there something more comforting? I (Chris) grew up with a dad who liked music from the '60s and '70s. To this day, that music brings up happy feelings because it reminds me of good times. However, when someone raises their voice, I get anxious because when I was a kid that sound usually meant something bad was about to happen.

c. What smells is your baby bonding with? When I (Chris) bonded with my grandmother she was usually baking. To this day, I associate the smell of baked goods with the happy memories of being at Grandma's house.

d. What voice tones does your baby hear? We need to realize that even if our anger or anxiety is unrelated to our babies, they tune in to what is in their environment. We need to keep the arguing out of earshot if possible.

2. These are good topics to discuss with others. Remember, there are no perfect parents! All of us have room for improvement, and the point here is to make simple and necessary changes to increase joy.

HABIT BUILDER #6—*Replace negative commands*

Start making an effort to use positive commands with your children. This will take some practice and effort but it's worth it!

1. Take some time for reflection on common ways you use negative commands. If you are unsure how you

use positive commands, ask other family members for some help on how you can transform negative commands into positive ones so that you can start to do it without thinking about it.

2. Make a list of common phrases, commands, and requests you use. Replace them with positive phrases instead. For example, I may find that I often say, "No, don't climb that cabinet! You will get hurt." So I want to replace this negative command with, "Stay on the floor. The floor is safer."

HABIT BUILDER #7—*Rest*

Chris writes, "Friends always told my wife, 'Nap when baby naps! Do not try to get work done during this time; you will need the rest.' This was wise. When parents have an infant at home, it is not the time to tackle housekeeping and gourmet meals that require time and energy you don't have. Use times of rest when baby is sleeping to rest and recharge your relational battery instead of trying to get a bunch of work done. You will be glad you rested!"

Growing joy doesn't happen when we're exhausted. Rest is a crucial foundation parents will need as they raise their babies to be joy-filled. Baby and rest do not often go together in the same sentence! However, small steps can go a long way to finding creative ways to rest and increase relational joy.

1. In what ways can you insert rest into your life?
2. Do you have trusted friends or family members who can come over to give you a breather to rest, get out for a walk, have a date night, etc.?

CHAPTER 4

Raising Joy-Filled Children

SOME OF MY (MARCUS'S) fondest childhood memories include riding bikes with my friends at the local park and "playing army." I'm old enough that World War II surplus was still available when I was young (my dad served in Patton's army). We had canteens, mess kits, backpacks, and other stuff we had bought from the army surplus store. We spent hours chasing bad guys and making the world safe for democracy. It was like a scene from Captain America.

Childhood is a time for adventure. It is a time for trying new things, expanding our skills, and overcoming our fears. As parents, we often feel the tension between giving our kids the freedom to do potentially dangerous things (like jumping off a rock into the lake or letting them sleep over at a friend's house) and the caution of keeping them safe and closely guarded. While we need to do things to keep our kids safe, our goal is not to wrap them in a bubble, but to help them learn how to experience hard things (emotional and physical) and bounce back. We want to build their capacity to do hard things at age-appropriate levels, as they begin to learn how to work for and wait for what is good.

The key to this is to give them age-appropriate tasks to do. You don't ask your five-year-old to go mow the lawn with a power mower. You give them little responsibilities at which they can succeed. If they can't succeed at the task, it is not age-appropriate. When I (Chris) was young, I helped with the dishes. As I grew older, it became my job, and my parents made me do the dishes after dinner before I could go play with my friends. My wife, Jen, has told me many times how grateful she is that my parents made me do the dishes. Now I am passing that discipline onto my children.

Joy-filled kids are ones who learn to do hard things and enjoy the satisfaction of their work. They learn the rhythm of rest, work, and play. Play is an important opportunity to practice relational skills. One important skill is learning when to stop. Children need to learn when it is time to stop teasing, to stop tickling, to stop yelling, and so on. Learning to give others a break even when we don't feel like quitting is a way of protecting them from our own impulses.

THE WISDOM YEARS

Childhood begins with weaning. We stop depending on Mom to feed us and learn to feed ourselves. It ends with puberty and the physical transformation that prepares young adults to become parents. Puberty has long been recognized as the transition point between childhood and the adult years. Recently, people have pointed out that the developing brain is not fully formed until age twenty-five, but that does not change the fact that once a child hits puberty that child could physically become a parent very quickly if they haven't learned how to work for and wait for what is good. These are years for learning wisdom.

Babies can act like fools. Let's face it. They have no idea what is good for them or bad for them. I remember coming home from a date with my wife to find my infant son crawling up the stairs with a butcher knife in his hands. He was giggling and happy with absolutely no clue that he could die if this didn't end well. The babysitter had made a pizza and used the butcher knife to cut it. Somehow, my active son had found a way to get it off the counter while everyone else was watching TV.

I tell this story because it illustrates the need for children to learn wisdom. My infant son had no idea that it was not good for him to crawl upstairs with a butcher knife in his hand. He thought it was the greatest thing ever! By the time our kids finish puberty (which usually happens around age thirteen) they need to be well practiced at taking care of themselves. This means they need to learn what is good for them and what is bad for them and how to anticipate consequences. Sometimes they learn through trial and error, and sometimes we need to instruct them and give consequences.

Let's start with a definition of wisdom. I find it interesting that the Hebrew word for wisdom (*chokmah*) also means skill. It captures the idea that a wise person is skilled at the art of living. This is part of what inspired the ABCD model of parenting. These four categories guide parents in knowing what skills they need to pass on to their kids.

There are two core elements to wisdom: discernment and discipline. Discernment is the ability to distinguish between what is good for me and what is bad for me— what will end well and what will end poorly. It includes the ability to distinguish between what is temporarily pleasurable and what is truly satisfying.

Helping our kids learn what is satisfying has many benefits.

1. They learn that some things are worth working for.
2. They learn that some things are worth waiting for.
3. It strengthens their identity to know what they find satisfying.
4. It helps them be more creative.
5. They learn they can add value to the world around them.

Something is satisfying when it makes you smile to relive the experience, or you can still feel the joy of the activity several days later. Recalling my days riding bikes with my friends still makes me smile. So do dozens of other memories from childhood like learning to water ski, the feel of hitting a home run in Little League, the sense of accomplishment at mastering my phonics book in school. As parents, we need to understand that satisfaction is not primarily about finishing a task. It is about the joy of sharing the experience with someone else who finds joy in it.

In order to grow wisdom and learn new skills, a child needs a blend of guidance and freedom. When I learned to water ski, my mom and dad couldn't teach me what to do because they had never done it. But they were in the boat rooting for me as a family friend taught me. I (Marcus) had never spent any time at a lake before and had no skills in swimming or any experience riding in a speedboat, let alone skiing. The first few attempts weren't pretty. I wiped out immediately. Then I got up for about ten seconds, hit a wave, and did a forward flip into the water. My parents kept encouraging me, and their friend kept instructing me, and the next time up, I made it all the way around the lake. The feeling of satisfaction was immense. Not only had I accomplished a task, but there were people celebrating it with me. That is a great recipe for developing disciplines relationally.

Discernment is primarily about recognizing what is satisfying. It is the foundation of wisdom. However, it needs to be paired with discipline. Discipline is the ability to work for and wait for what is good or satisfying. One of the words I often heard from my parents was "excellence." They instilled in their kids the ideal of doing our best and taking the time needed to do things with excellence. Because my parents invested in helping us learn to work hard at what we did, all of us kids got used to success. We had to deal with failure along the way, but the disciplines instilled by our parents made success seem normal. For example, my (Marcus's) mom loved art. She loved to help us with our art homework. She was especially good at portraits. She helped us with proportions, shading, and other techniques. As a result, we tended to win most of the art contests we entered. Our mother took the time to relationally help us develop the disciplines to do our work with excellence. This was also the case with music, academics, sports, and other pursuits. It wasn't overbearing. They weren't saying, "You better succeed or else." They were saying, "Do your best. Work hard at this and we'll see what happens." They also took the time to celebrate our successes, comfort us in our failures, and make sure we "got back to work" the next day.

To help our children grow wisdom and develop the maturity that helps them do hard things and still live with joy, we need to understand how to apply the four habits of raising joy-filled kids during the child years. The rest of the chapter will help with this.

ATTUNING WITH CHILDREN

Desiring to create some special memories with my (Chris's) younger son, Andrew, I saw an opportunity when a local church was offering a pinewood derby competition. Andrew was very excited about this opportunity, so I agreed to help him build a fast car for the big race. As a child, my uncle and I worked on a pinewood derby car, which turned into a special memory I have always cherished. "What better opportunity to do something fun and meaningful?" I thought. Together, my son and I worked on fashioning, forming, and painting the small wooden car. On race day, Andrew had the opportunity to race his fast-looking car. Much to our surprise, the car finished last in every race. I had failed to add the proper weight to the car, which made it too light. The oversight meant the car did not move quickly.

The look of disappointment on Andrew's face after the race was crushing, but this moment turned into an opportunity to learn from the mistake and increase wisdom, and I realized I needed to share my son's disappointment. I shared sadness over the mistake, attuned with Andrew who was feeling deflated, and together we returned to joy, focusing on what was fun and meaningful about the process. Through the failure we learned a valuable lesson we could put into practice next time. By staying connected with Andrew, I was able to convey to him that he was not alone in his sadness. Even though the car failed to win a race, it was an opportunity for us to bond and grow together. The key in this example is that I did not put pressure on Andrew to attune with *my* feelings. I did not justify my mistake or make excuses to minimize the problem; rather, I focused on attuning with my son. We felt sadness together and stayed relationally connected. As children experience attunement from their parents and caregivers on a regular basis, they learn to recover on their own when things go wrong.

> *Even though the car failed to win a race, it was an opportunity for us to bond and grow together.*

Parents attune with their children by giving their full attention to them when they are in need. We do this through our facial expressions, tone of voice, appropriate touch, and the words we use. Attunement is generally the first step in problem solving and engaging in teaching moments. As parents, we are usually busy and want to resolve problems quickly. Because of this, we often don't take the time to attune to our child's emotional state before we start telling them what to do or try to fix their problems.

If my daughter is playing happily and I walk into the room without attuning to her emotional state and simply start barking orders or expressing how upset I am that she did not do something I asked her to do, my daughter is not apt to learn that she has done something wrong or that she needs to obey. Instead, she will learn that I can be scary and unpredictable; that I need to be managed. If I ask my son to put his toys away before he starts watching TV, but he doesn't do it, my job is to handle the situation like an adult. That means I don't come in yelling or shaming or scolding and change the entire atmosphere in the room because I am upset. I attune. I notice what is going on and that my son is happy. I might comment, "I see you are watching one of your favorite shows." Then I get to the problem. "Did you forget that I asked you to pick up your toys?" The order is important: attune first, deal with the problem second. Sometimes our children aren't being rebellious; they just haven't learned discipline yet.

One of the most common mistakes parents make is the failure to attune *before* problem solving. Mastering this habit helps keep relationships bigger than problems while still dealing with the problems.

BUILDING BOUNCE WITH CHILDREN

One of the most important tasks children need to learn as they build their maturity is how to bounce back from upsetting emotions. In technical terms, this is often called emotional regulation. We regulate our emotions by remembering who we are and how it is like us to act when we have certain emotions, and by practicing the skills we have learned (like VCR) on how to return to joy from our distress.

At the infant stage all emotional regulation is external. The infant can't regulate their emotions at all. Parents, or someone else external to the child, have to do the work of helping them quiet and recover. At the child stage, we begin to practice "co-regulation." This means we start working with our kids to help them learn how to regulate their own emotions. We help children learn to Validate and Comfort themselves by guiding them through each step so they can self-validate, self-comfort, and learn to Recover with our oversight. We do not expect them to have this skill learned as they enter childhood, but our goal is to guide them through the process again and again, so they learn to self-regulate without our help by the time they are adults. Children who have not been trained to regulate their own emotions by the time they go through puberty are going to have a much harder time navigating the transition. The process of regulating at different stages looks like this:

- Infant—external regulation
- Child—co-regulation
- Adult—self-regulation

One of the core characteristics of moving into the child stage of life is the increasing ability to communicate with words. So one of the ways we help our children build bounce is by helping them put words to their feelings. As infants, we met them in their big emotions, shared those emotions, and helped them quiet without ex-

> *What we fear is not so much pain as it is getting stuck in the emotions that pain causes.*

plaining what was happening. In the child years, we do all of the same things, but add words to the process.

During the child years, we need to introduce our children to feeling words like *joy*, *peace*, *shame*, *sadness*, *anger*, *fear*, *disgust*, and *despair*. We help them identify when they are feeling these emotions by validating those emotions and putting words to them. If a person gets really good at bouncing back from negative emotions, those emotions stop being scary and just become part of life that you have to navigate.

On the other hand, any emotion we don't master becomes a reason for fear that robs life of its sense of adventure. In many ways, what we fear is not so much pain as it is getting stuck in the emotions that pain causes. If we are afraid we will feel despair, and we know we can't handle despair, we start to fear any situation that might cause feelings of hopelessness. Feeling alone in negative emotions creates attachment pain, the pain of loss. Once we feel stuck and alone this creates difficult circumstances for the brain to process distressing emotions. If we are only good at bouncing back from one of the "big six" negative emotions (shame, sadness, anger, fear, disgust, despair), it means we are going to be afraid of the other five and our world will shrink as we avoid more and more relationships and opportunities.

My (Marcus's) coauthor for the book *Building Bounce: How to Grow Emotional Resilience* is art therapist and Christian counselor Stefanie Hinman. In the book she talks about a day when her daughter experienced rejection on the playground at school. As a mom, everything in her wanted to protect her daughter from that kind of pain. She wanted to "Bubble Wrap" her kids and make sure they never had to deal with such difficult emotions again. But as she reflected on the situation, she realized that instead of Bubble-Wrapping her kids, she needed to help them build their emotional immune systems. The goal wasn't to make sure her kids never felt the pain of rejection. The goal was to build "immunity" to the pain by learning how to bounce back from it. In fact, dealing with a certain amount of such pain actually grows our compassion for others who experience it. By helping them build bounce, her kids wouldn't have to be afraid of the playground even if some of the kids were occasionally mean.[1]

There are limits to this, of course. We aren't saying to

ignore bullying. We aren't abandoning our kids to difficult situations and telling them to toughen up. We attune with our kids and comfort them and help them participate in the process so that they learn the skill for themselves.

CORRECTING CHILDREN WITH CARE

The key to correcting children well is remaining relational. Remaining relational is all about mastering an important brain function we call the "Joy Switch."[2] When this switch is on, remaining relational is easy, but when it is off it can be virtually impossible to remain relational. There are relational circuits in our brain that allow us to act like ourselves and connect relationally with others. When these circuits get too dim or turn off altogether, we don't act like ourselves. In an instant we can go from friendly and engaging to shut down, sulking, or scary.

Have you ever been in a conversation that was going well until you got triggered? Then, all of a sudden it was like you turned into a different person. This has happened to me (Marcus) on many occasions. As a parent, I can sometimes get so focused on the problem my child has caused that my Joy Switch shuts off. When that happens, I do not attune to my child; I just want the problem to get fixed and my life to get easier. Here is a short list of what happens when the Joy Switch shuts down.

- We lose curiosity. This usually happens because we think we have our kids all figured out. As a result, we lose our curiosity about how our child feels or what they think. We just want them to comply.
- We lose appreciation. In the moment, while we are upset, we don't remember what we appreciate about our child. In fact, we can begin to see our child as a problem to be managed or an enemy to be defeated.
- We lose kindness. When the Joy Switch goes off, I don't feel like being kind anymore. In fact, I can get mean if I am not careful.
- We lose eye contact, unless it is to stare our kid down.

Learning to recognize when your Joy Switch is off is a crucial parenting skill. If we have lost curiosity, appreciation, kindness, and eye contact (which spells CAKE to make it easier to remember), we will not correct with care. Therefore, the first step in correcting with care is to make sure your relational circuits are on. You do this by taking a moment to recognize they are off, disconnecting briefly until you can find some curiosity, appreciation, and kindness, then making eye contact and attuning to your child.

I (Chris) can remember walking into my child's room and seeing that the job I had given them to do had been neglected in order to play a video game. I have handled this type of problem in two very different ways: with my Joy Switch on or with my Joy Switch off. When my Switch is off, I lead with my anger and my fixation on the problem. I let my child know how upset I am and how disappointed I am that the job has not been done. When my Switch is on, I do not lead with my upset emotions

Our goal in correcting with care is forming character, not just correcting behavior.

but by synchronizing with my child's emotions. I might say something like, "I see you are enjoying your video game. That's not what I sent you here to do, is it? Do you remember what you were supposed to do?" By reading his emotional state and leading with curiosity I kept the situation relational.

Our goal in correcting with care is forming character, not just correcting behavior. You may recall that at the infant level, toddlers can't process a negative command. Therefore, we need to learn how to give positive instructions to our little ones. As we move into the child stage, correcting with care looks different. You can think of the process as a "correction sandwich" in which you put the problem between two slices of relational bread.[3] The goal is to keep the relationship bigger than the problem as we correct our children. First, we will introduce the model;

then we will troubleshoot a few common issues that arise.

Let's say a child is upset because he wants to play video games instead of doing chores. This is a case where we need to correct with care. Using the correction sandwich approach might look like this.

1. Relate. Relate by attuning to your child's emotions rather than leading with your own. We might say, "I see you are upset that I told you to clean your room when you wanted to play. I know cleaning is not as fun as playing games on your tablet, but . . ." What comes after the word "but" is the second step. The first step is attuning and getting the conversation off to a relational start.

Another tool that helps keep problems relational is curiosity. Because we are often sure we have our kids figured out (which we probably do), we often skip asking them questions to draw them out and guide them. You can practice this skill by starting sentences with the words, "I'm curious . . ." or "I'm wondering . . ." So you might ask, "I'm wondering what stopped you from doing what I asked. Did you get distracted?"

2. Resolve. Identify and resolve the problem. Explain what needs correcting. If needed, we can give a few options on how to solve the problem. To go back to our conversation from the first step, it might look like this.

"I see you are upset that I told you to clean your room when you wanted to play. I know cleaning is not as fun as playing games on your tablet, but work needs to come before play. Get your job done and you can play after you finish."

At this point most kids push back. They are going to look for a strategy to get what they want. If one works, they will return to it again and again. Here are some common pushbacks.

- Cuteness—They may try to charm you into letting them have their way. They may bat their eyes and say, "Please!!!" as they play on your emotions and hope you give in.
- Tantrums—This can happen on a scale that ranges from pouting to yelling and breaking things. "This isn't fair. You let Olivia play her game. You never let me do what I want."
- Shame—The goal is to manipulate you by making you second-guess yourself. Sometimes we give in just to relieve the tension. "You never let me have any fun. You ruin everything! I hate you."
- Bargaining—"Just give me five more minutes. If you let me play now, I'll get this done later, I promise."
- Arguing—If you offer a reason for why they need to obey, they will find one point in what you said and attack it. "Work doesn't need to come before play. That's stupid. I can get both things done before lunch."

> *You don't want to set a precedent of needing to win an argument before your kids will obey you.*

You can probably think of many other strategies kids use to get their way. If they discover that one or two of these strategies work, they will use it again and again until they become experts at the art of manipulation.

One way to avoid the whole argument process in the childhood stage is to require obedience now with the promise of an explanation later. This doesn't work with adults, but it is effective with children. When your child asks, "Why? Why do I have to do this?" you can promise them an explanation later—after they obey. You don't want to set a precedent of needing to win an argument before your kids will obey you. We need to learn to say things like, "You finish your chores first, and we'll talk about it later."

3. Restore. Restore the relationship. The "correction sandwich" process concludes by making sure the child knows their relationship with you is secure. This may not happen until after they have obeyed or have received consequences. But the idea is to make sure that you end with a sense of having a reconnected relationship. Our goal isn't simply to get the child to obey, but to grow their maturity, which includes modeling how to deal with problems (even disobedience) relationally.

A word on consequences. We need to make sure consequences fit the action. You don't ground a kid for a month for talking back to you. You don't invent consequences in the heat of the moment. Instead, it is important to establish clear expectations of what the consequences will be before you start. It can also be helpful to postpone pronouncing consequences until you have time to think (and calm down). You might say, "I am going to go think about this for a minute and I'll let you know what is going to happen when I return or when Mom gets home."

Restoring the relationship may happen at bedtime. Recently one of my (Chris's) sons said, "I wish I had parents who would let me do whatever I want." I was able to validate that feeling then use it as a teaching moment. I said, "It's because we love you that we correct and guide you. If we didn't care about you, we'd let you do whatever you wanted. We wouldn't care. But we do care because we love you." I (Marcus) often told my kids, "I want you to be successful in life. There are some paths that lead to success and some that don't. The path you are on does not lead to success; therefore I need to correct you before you get going too far in the wrong direction."

When he was in early elementary school, our (Marcus and Brenda's) son told us he had been cheating on his math homework. To his credit, we would not have known if he had not confessed. We practiced the correction sandwich approach. Relate: We sat down with him and did our best to attune to his emotions. He felt shame and fear, so we validated those emotions. Resolve: After attuning and validating, we then attempted to resolve the problem by showing curiosity to find out what actually happened and why. We then took a break and came back with the decision that his consequence would be double the math homework for a week. Restore: We wrapped up by giving him a hug and letting him know we appreciated his honesty and loved him.

We also let him know this wouldn't change our plans for going out to eat together as a family, and I promised not to bring this up while we were out having fun. The correction sandwich approach kept the relationship bigger than the problem. We have had to revisit this event a few times since then, not to shame him, but to see what his feelings were now that some time had gone by. Even though everything seemed fine at the time, there have been a few opportunities to strengthen our relationship by demonstrating curiosity and connection over his emotions since that event.

HEALTHY SHAME

As we saw in the last chapter, healthy shame is a corrective reminder that tells us when our actions and behaviors do not adequately reflect our identity. It provides us with an opportunity to correct our behavior, so it more fully reflects who we are. Just like the infant stage, we use our face, voice, and body language to communicate that we are not happy with what is happening. The difference at the child stage is that we start to help them put words to what they are experiencing. For example, our sons (Chris and Jen's) were playing indoors and things got a little too rough. While wrestling around, energy levels spiked to the point where one boy became angry and kicked his brother. This caused the recipient of the kick to start crying. We stepped in with a healthy shame message, saying, "Oh no! This is hurting your brother. That is not good behavior. You are a kind brother who is normally loving and gentle. Do you see his face right now; is he happy with you? No? Okay, how can we change that? Do you have any ideas?"

Notice we didn't just blast the behavior. We invited him to relationally participate in the solution. Our son admitted he needed to apologize, and he told his brother he was sorry. Within a few short moments the two were laughing together again. Joy had been restored. By correcting with care, we were able to teach the lesson that it is like us to be gentle and tender toward others. Our goal was not just to resolve the problem but to model how to resolve conflicts so they would have that skill as they got older.

Toxic shame would have simply said, "Stop being stupid! What do you think you are doing to your brother?" Maybe a punishment would follow like "Now go to your room until you can stop being a bully." This toxic shame message would attack his identity and leave him relationally alone to deal with his emotions.

DEVELOPING DISCIPLINES
RELATIONALLY WITH CHILDREN

There is no point trying to get a child under age five to do hard things or learn hard lessons.[4] Their brains and emotional capacity aren't ready for that yet. We often traumatize our little ones with well-intentioned but misguided attempts to help them grow up too soon. Instead, we need to start with small steps that match a child's stage of development.

Once we get to the childhood stage, we want to give our children tasks that stretch them just a little bit. In this stage, struggle leads to growth as children learn to do hard things with our supervision. I have a friend whose dad thought it would be a good bonding experience to have him help him work on cars. But the boy was only six. His dad would ask for specific kinds of tools without any sense that his son had no idea what the names of the tools were. His dad would get angry with him and, instead of a happy bonding experience, it became traumatic for the child. It would have been better at that age to have the boy collect and organize nuts and bolts or to begin teaching him the names of tools and quizzing him on them. The dad was not attuned to his son's overwhelm and pushed too hard. Attunement lets us know if we are pushing our kids too hard. When we see they are in distress, we need to take a break and reevaluate our approach.

When my daughter was eleven, I (Marcus) decided to build a deck and let her help. I was using power tools and spent hours on the project. I didn't expect her to contribute significantly to the process or work on the job the whole time. Instead, I gave her little tasks to do like drawing lines on the wood where I had the T-bar positioned, collecting and organizing the materials, and handing me tools I would need. I also let her hammer nails now and then. She participated at an age-appropriate level. Now that she is an adult, she could handle more. We might even reverse roles. I would simply walk her through what to do and serve as her assistant while she built the deck.

One of the keys to knowing when you are being age-appropriate with what you are doing is by attuning to your child's sense of overwhelm. For example, if I want my daughter to practice the piano for an hour, but she gets overwhelmed after ten minutes, I need to notice that and build some rest into her routine. I may still have her practice for an hour, but every ten to fifteen minutes I might offer her something to drink or have her walk around the room once or tell me a joke. Gradually, her capacity to work longer than ten to fifteen minutes consecutively will grow. In the same way, I wouldn't tell my six-year-old to go clean his room, as if that is a perfectly clear concept to a child of that age. I will go with him to the room and do the various chores with him, looking for signs of overwhelm along the way and taking breaks as needed. Once you get to the point where the child says, "I can do this without your help," you can give them some space, review their work, and celebrate their successes.

There are several goals in helping our children develop disciplines relationally.

- It helps us build a healthy relationship.
- It equips our children with skills they will need in life.
- It expands the child's world.
- It grows the child's confidence.
- It reinforces the child's identity.

You can probably think of other benefits as well. Passing on disciplines in relational, age-appropriate ways is a very important habit for raising joy-filled kids.

WISDOM AND STORYTELLING

As we wrap up this chapter, let's circle back to the idea of wisdom. One of the ways we help our children grow both their wisdom and maturity is through storytelling. It is especially important for them to know the story of their family. They need to know the good and the bad—at age-appropriate levels. We want them to understand their place in the larger story of life.

I sometimes playfully called my son "Benjamin, the son of Marcus, the son of Timothy, the son of Ward"—the latest in the great line of Warner men. I would then tell him stories about his grandfather and how he served in MASH units in Patton's army during World War II. We looked at his medals and other items he brought back from the war (including a Nazi armband from an enemy prisoner). I told him about his great-grandfather Ward who was a plasterer and raised a family with eight kids during the Great Depression. He learned how Ward's dad (also a plasterer) had gambled away the down payment on a large job and then died unexpectedly, leaving the family in great debt just as the Depression struck. I used the story to help him understand the importance of being wise with money and avoiding the temptation to get rich quick.

Knowing these and many other stories about his family history creates a sense of identity and purpose in the world. For his fifteenth birthday, we gave him a framed family crest. He was in a Latin class at the time and enjoyed ancient Roman history, so we had the family motto written in Latin on the crest—*non nobis tantum nati*, which means, "Not for ourselves alone are we born." It is a wonderful call to service. To reinforce the sense

Our kids need to know some of the good and bad about us.

of identity on his sixteenth birthday, we gave him a replica of a gladius (the sword of a Roman soldier) to put on display in his room.

Not only do we want our kids to know their place in our multigenerational family story, but they need to know some of the good and bad about us as well. It is important to tell stories of times you failed and experienced shame as well as times when you were the hero. Telling our kids stories of how we failed at dealing with hard things can be a jumpstart to explaining what we should have done. Such stories reinforce the idea that nobody is perfect and that you can't grow if you never fail. Chris often makes it a point to talk to his sons about times he messed up, so his sons both understand the errors their father made, but also learn *how to stay relational* while navigating problems. These examples become an important part of the legacy we leave to our children so they learn failure does not have the final word. Failures are prime opportunities for growth and wisdom.

How well you can tell your life story has a significant impact on how well you attach to your children. We can predict the quality of a child's attachment to a parent by how well the parent can tell a coherent, autobiographical life story. The process of telling this story in addition to sharing our mental and emotional states with our children helps build strong attachments. Learning how to tell our life story in a coherent way creates a path for our children to be able to see their connection to that story and find their place in the world.[5]

THE PATH AHEAD

Raising joy-filled children builds on the previous stage of life, the infant stage. We build on this foundation of joy by looking for opportunities to help our children grow wisdom that comes from life experience and a shared reality with other people who listen, attune, and share joy together. We learn to keep relationships bigger than problems by using correction sandwiches to correct with care, which focuses on the relationship and addresses what is robbing joy. We continue to monitor and pay attention to our children's emotional capacity so we develop disciplines relationally with our children by noticing what is manageable and reasonable to expect. We focus on increasing shared responsibility with small steps and avoid placing too much weight on a fragile foundation.

HABIT BUILDER #8—*Satisfying projects*

We want to teach our kids the satisfaction of a job well done. Doing puzzles, building models, creating art, or playing an instrument are just a few ways we can bond over projects with our kids. Consider doing a small, fun project with your child. You want to work on something with your child that is satisfying and meaningful for both of you. It should be something the child is excited to do with you! The key words there are "with you."

- As a word of caution, do not try taking on something that is too big, will take too long, or will be drawn out over time. These sorts of projects can backfire. Pick something simple that your child is excited about doing.
- Use this opportunity to build some joy together and make special memories that will last a lifetime.

HABIT BUILDER #9—*Practice sandwich corrections*

In this chapter, we learned about sandwich corrections. If this approach is new to you, your brain will most likely focus on the problem instead of the relationship. This means some practice is needed in order to change the way your brain thinks about and manages problems! Here is a good opportunity for growth.

1. Pick one problem you had to address this past week. Using the three-step correction sandwich model, write out how you could have handled that situation.
   a. First, identify the emotion your child was feeling. How could you have validated that emotion?

    b. Second, how could you have used curiosity to draw out solutions or prevented arguments? How would you word your response?

    c. Third, what would ending the situation with a good relationship have looked like? Write out a sample closing statement that affirms their identity, your love, and your desire for relational connection.

2. This will take time and practice, so do this with several "problems" you are navigating and practice sharing these with your spouse or a friend. Once you feel confident you have this sequence down, practice expressing these sandwich corrections with your children.

HABIT BUILDER #10—*Share highlights from your life*

What were some valuable, meaningful moments you want your children to know about? Be sure to keep these all age-appropriate. A twelve-year-old can understand much more than a five-year-old, so adjust accordingly.

- What mistakes did your family make when you were young, and how has this helped you increase in wisdom?
- How did your family grow joy when you were younger?
- Try to make your story clear, coherent, and compelling.

Everyone likes stories! Use highlights from your life to practice storytelling as an opportunity to connect relationally, teach wisdom, and grow joy.

CHAPTER 5

Joy-Filled Adults

AS A YOUNG ADULT, I (Chris) got a paper route. That used to be a popular job for older kids and young adults. At first, my father helped me make sure the newspapers got delivered to the right houses and went with me as I collected the payments from the families. Over time, I took over the entire process myself. I even recruited friends to help, especially when I had to stuff all of the extra inserts into the Sunday edition. My dad helped me learn to do hard things. I often had to work in the early morning while it was still dark. It could be snowing, sleeting, or raining, and I still had to get the newspapers delivered. It was a big route that demanded a lot of bike riding. There were even some mean dogs that needed to be handled. But the reward came every month when I collected the payments and got my salary.

The highlight of the year was Christmas bonus time.

People often gave me cookies, treats, and extra cash. I was learning how to work like an adult. I learned the importance of being on time, working hard, enduring hardship well, and taking responsibility. All of this helped to prepare me for life in the adult world.

During the child years, a parent is like a coach. We teach skills, give instructions, expect obedience, and dole out consequences. Once a child reaches puberty, the world changes for them and for us. Our role becomes that of a mentor. We need to become trusted guides as our children learn to stand on their own as an adult in a world of adults. Instead of simply telling them what to do, we discuss things with them. We help our adult children think through situations and scenarios as they figure out how to handle life in new ways. As they continue to live with us, we establish rules but seek agreement on those rules and what the consequences will be for breaking agreed-upon guidelines. As the stage of life changes for our kids and they become adults, our approach to parenting needs to mature as well.

PUBERTY—THE BEGINNING OF LIFE AS AN ADULT

The physical changes that come with puberty reorganize and destroy many parts of the brain in a process known as neural organization and synaptic pruning.[1] Unused connections in the thinking and processing areas of the child's brain are thinned out while other connections are strengthened.[2] This means grey matter is thinned while white matter is strengthened. The grey matter in the brain is what allows plasticity. If you are not familiar with that term, it means your brain can grow new connections and develop new skills. The good news about grey matter and brain plasticity is that we all have the ability to learn new things and grow new skills for as long as we live. A child's brain is mostly grey matter, which means they learn new skills and information easily. White matter is related to forming habits. White matter forms as pathways in the brain develop and neurons link together. These neural pathways get wrapped in white matter through a process called myelination. As white matter gets more fully developed it sends messages through our brain at superfast speeds. It is the superfast transmission of information that creates habits.

For example, it is impossible for the average person to hit a Major League fastball. Grey matter cannot process information fast enough to read and react to what is happening. To someone who is not used to the speed, it will feel like they are about to get killed when they see the ball coming at them with such velocity. It is white matter that has developed through years of practice that allows a major league batter to have any chance of hitting a pitch traveling over 90 miles per hour. When it comes to raising joy-filled kids, our goal is to instill habits that allow our kids to react to life with a level of maturity and resilience that only comes with lots of practice.

The point of a habit is to do things automatically. Our habits determine our character. If we build good habits, we will strengthen our character and it will show up automatically. If we build bad habits, it weakens our character and those habits will show up before we even realize what is happening. If our children haven't learned the lessons of childhood before puberty, it is going to be much harder to learn them afterwards.

The point of a habit is to do things automatically.

There is a use-it-or-lose-it element to the "housecleaning" processes that happen in the brain at puberty. Skills that are used can grow stronger after puberty. However, skills and abilities we do not use much will be weakened or lost altogether. If a child did not learn how to return to joy from hard emotions (if they did not experience enough of the VCR process), it is going to be harder to learn that skill as an adult. If a child did not learn how to ride a bike, play an instrument, or speak French, it is going to be harder after puberty, because the part of the brain designed to learn such things gets weakened, if not completely wiped away. As parents, it is important to guide our children to understand the road map that's ahead of them as they go through puberty. We need to help them interpret the many changes going on in their bodies and brains.

One of the reasons the experience of puberty can be traumatic for kids is because they reached the end of childhood without being well practiced in the skills needed to take care of themselves or regulate their own emotions. They haven't mastered the child-level skills they needed to learn. As a result, the increased demands of entering an adult world will be overwhelming. We hear a lot these days about young adults living in a constant state of overwhelm and anxiety—seeking safe spaces, sensitive to microaggressions,[3] and often struggling to handle "adulting."

Many young adults face this sense of overwhelm by refusing to grow up—and many parents let them. The teen years become a second childhood in which we hope our kids will learn lessons and build skills they did not develop as children. This is not a great plan for success. The longer this goes on, the less prepared for the adult world our kids will be.

As our kids enter the adult years, they need several forms of guidance from us as parents.

1. We need to provide a rite of passage for our adult kids.[4] The purpose of a rite of passage is to say goodbye to childhood and celebrate the beginning of life as an adult. In most cultures, this happens around age thirteen. Catholics and some Protestant denominations have confirmation. Jewish communities have bar and bat mitzvahs. Many Latin American countries have quinceaneras in celebration of a girl's fifteenth birthday. Nearly all ancient cultures observed a rite of passage to mark the transition from child to adult for both boys and girls. In America, this practice is not nearly as common and is likely a symptom of the overall decline in maturity in our culture. An effective rite of passage has a few key elements.

- A good rite of passage requires a child to complete appropriate challenges. There needs to be a sense that childhood tasks have been mastered. There also needs to be a recognition that they are ready to face adult challenges. This looks different in different parts of the world, but it usually has something to do with proving that you can handle an important task related to survival as an adult.

   For example, you might take your kid camping. Their challenge is to set up the camp, build the fire, cook the dinner, and supervise the outing. Obviously, in order to do this, these skills would have had to have been learned and practiced many times prior to the event. The point is to demonstrate their capacity to handle the responsibility. The rite of passage should fit the child, their interests and skills. Perhaps it is preparing a fancy dinner for a group of guests or submitting a piece of art for a contest. Whatever you decide, you want it to be meaningful and something that both showcases and stretches their skill set.

- A good rite of passage requires a child to spend time with older members of the community and experience life in the adult world. Part of stepping out of the world of children into the world of adults is building relationships with adults. Using our camping analogy, other adults may go camping with you prior to the rite of passage and participate in teaching skills like identifying poison oak or berries that aren't safe to eat. Or a child getting ready to make a profession of faith might work with an adult teacher or group leader in her church, studying the basics of the faith. The point is to teach kids how to look adults in the eyes, have meaningful conversations, and build connection through the mentoring process.

- A good rite of passage requires a ceremony of celebration in which the child is welcomed into the world of adults by adults. Thus, you might invite all of the people who helped to teach your child the skills they have mastered to come on the outing. At a campfire ceremony, each one could pass on some wisdom and share some strength they recognize in your child. The participation of these adults helps to establish a new group identity for our kids that says, "I am an adult. I am strong. I am ready. I belong." Or, on a tamer level, parents could invite adult teachers and mentors to a graduation party for their child.

2. We need to help our adult kids bond with peers and form a group identity. Part of the brain change that happens at puberty affects the identity center of the brain. Instead of looking to parents for their sense of identity, teens begin to look at their peers to determine who they are. This isn't just a choice they make. It is the result of new wiring in their brains. For a young adult, the key to their identity is the answer to the question "Who are my people?" Am I a jock? Am I a nerd? Am I popular? Am I an outsider? Am I part of the party crowd? Who are my people?

A good friend of mine (Marcus's) found his identity with the party crowd during the teen years. He had just moved to a new city and didn't know anyone. One day, he stood up to a bully at the school and immediately became a hero to all the outsiders who had felt picked on. He started getting invited to parties that centered on doing drugs and experimenting with sex. His identity came from his group. He thought of himself as a "bad boy" who didn't care about school, just the next pleasurable experience he could find. Eventually, his life turned around. He got a girl pregnant and found himself a parent. Clearly something had to change. The good news was that he came from a strong family who walked with him through these challenges. He also returned to his roots of faith. He had grown up in a Bible-believing family, walked away from that, but found his way back. The combination of reconnecting with his family and his faith got him on a new path that led to a new sense of who his people were and how it was like him to act. Today, he and his wife are raising their own set of joy-filled kids.

If a young adult feels like he or she doesn't fit in anywhere, it will affect their sense of self. One of the reasons so many young adults struggle with depression is that they don't have a healthy sense of attachment to their group.

We can't always control the identity group our kids choose. We can help. However, we have to give our newly adult children the space and time to bond with their peers. This, of course, involves a certain amount of trust on our part. The good news is, if we have been consistent during the child years in helping our kids learn wisdom, we usually have a good attachment already established with them. Giving our young adults space doesn't mean we abandon them to the new world they are in. Our goal is to stay relationally available so we can answer the door when they knock.

3. We need to help our adult kids connect with mentors. At the adult stage it is very important that we as parents not be the only mentors in our kids' lives. We want to encourage them to connect with coaches, teachers, pastors, and other adults who provide models for them to observe. Sometimes these models are good and sometimes they are not. Part of mentoring your young adult child is interacting with them about what they like and don't like in the people they see. Helping them identify what that means about who they are and what they value becomes crucial. At the adult stage, it is often other adults who become the dominant influence in someone's life. As parents, we have to learn to be okay with this, but to stay relational enough to be able to interact with new ideas and observations about life.

Part of mentoring involves giving increasing responsibility for important tasks that impact the community. Both leadership and service opportunities are important for young adults to be able to grow in what it means to add value to their people. I watched this as my daughter was given not only important roles in her school plays, but significant responsibility for directing the younger students as well. After several years in drama, she began volunteering to help direct local school plays. She also became deeply involved in storytelling and writing. Eventually, she formed bonds with other adults who shared these interests. They became her people. All of this helped grow her capacity and confidence to interact in the world of adults as an adult.

4. We need to train our adult kids how to use their power for good.[5] My kids both loved the various Spider Man movies from Marvel. In one scene, Uncle Ben tells Peter Parker, "With great power comes great responsibility." It is a really good line at two levels (at least). First, Uncle Ben is affirming that Peter has power. It is important for us as parents (and mentors to others) to empower our adult kids and help them see and understand various ways in which they are powerful. It can be powerful to be a friend to someone else. It can be powerful to recognize a need and meet it with empathy. It can be powerful to write well. It can be powerful to strategize creatively. It can be powerful to excel in sports. One of the key questions our adult kids need to get answered by us is this: "Do you think I am powerful? If so, how?"

Second, Uncle Ben's words point us to the goal of using power for good. In this sense, we want to guide our adult children to make an imprint on the world for good and not just to live for their own pleasure. We want to dream with them and evaluate options with them in ways that help them understand both that there are things about them that are powerful and that they need to first protect others from that power, and second, use that power to make a difference in the world—not just for their own personal gain.

One of the key elements of using power for good is protecting others from our power. Adults have to learn when enough is enough. By this time, we learn to recognize when others need a break, when they have boundaries we need to respect, and when we are overwhelming them. These skills are strengthened in the adult stage as we practice with our peers. People who do not learn how to protect others from themselves become predatory. They learn to see life as all about winning and losing, rather than relational strength. In reality, these people are not so much "becoming" predatory as they are failing to learn the skills to curb their predatory nature.

All babies are born "predators."[6] That may sound strange, but essentially it means that they see the world as something to consume. Everything is potential food. This, of course, ensures their survival, but part of maturing is learning that not everything is out there for our pleasure and consumption. Learning to work for what is satisfying, wait for what is good, and help others experience what is good are maturity skills that curb predatory behavior. Those who don't mature and don't learn such skills become dangerous to themselves and others. One of the benefits of raising mature, joy-filled kids is that they tend to be less predatory—and that is good for everyone.

Sometimes we think we have our kids all figured out, so we don't really listen.

With these factors in mind, let's turn our attention to the four habits of raising joy-filled kids and explore how they apply at the adult stage of life.

ATTUNING WITH OUR ADULT KIDS

Adults still need a good hug—but at this stage we offer the hug, or it should be invited. We continue to use VCR just like we would for a spouse or a peer. Now at the adult stage, one of the goals of attunement is to become a sounding board for problem-solving. This starts with active listening in which we mirror feelings and demonstrate curiosity about their feelings and perspectives. Curiosity is a major part of attunement at the adult stage of life. Sometimes we think we have our kids all figured out, so we don't really listen. We feel like we know what they think and how they feel and what they should be doing, so we don't take the time to display authentic curiosity about what is important to their heart.

Curiosity and attunement naturally lead to helping our adult children think through how it is like them to handle the situations they face. We help them weigh options, evaluating pros and cons, but we also remind them how their heart is wired and how to let that shine through in the way they handle their relationships and problems.

Heart characteristics. Helping our adult children identify their heart characteristics also makes it easier for them to identify who their people are. The clearer they are on their heart characteristics, the more they will find themselves looking for friends with common values and not just common interests.

Here are some examples of what we mean by heart characteristics.

- Justice—I want to see everyone treated fairly.
- Mercy—I don't want to see anyone suffer.
- Compassion—I want to share the suffering of others, so they don't feel alone.

- Leadership—I want to guide my people to a satisfying destination.
- Service—I want to help make burdens lighter.
- Friendship—I want people to know I care.
- Teaching—I want to help people learn information that will make their life better.
- Coaching—I want to train people in skills that will make their life better.
- Organization—I want to make life easier and more satisfying by bringing order out of chaos.

There are many more heart characteristics that could be mentioned.[7] These are just examples. However, helping your child understand what their primary heart characteristics are adds clarity to their sense of identity and their sense of direction in knowing how to act like themselves. As with every stage of parenting, attunement comes before guidance.

BUILDING BOUNCE WITH OUR ADULT KIDS

When our kids become adults, ideally self-regulation is not a new skill. They should be fairly good at regulating their own emotions. There are two key issues we want to explore when it comes to building bounce at the adult stage of life.

1. Our adult kids need to focus not only on bouncing back from their own emotions but participating in help-

ing their group bounce back from difficult emotions. As with other elements of adult maturity, this principle is based on the idea that children take care of one person—themselves—while adults need to take care of two people at the same time. At the adult stage, our kids should learn to practice VCR (validate, comfort, recover) with their friends. They should increase their ability to attune to others while still taking care of their own emotional needs. This is an important adult skill. We all need to learn how to help without getting sucked in so far that we can't be okay emotionally until someone resolves their situation.

2. We help our adult kids bounce back from hard emotions through attunement and mutual problem solving. We no longer solve problems for our children at this level. We help them think through solutions and scenarios and determine a path forward for themselves.

As adults, the next step is for them to learn how to help others in their group regulate their emotions. As they learn to read the body language of their friends and attune with them, they help others in their group remain relational and act like themselves in the midst of challenging circumstances. After several years of attuning and comforting with their friends, it will be much easier for our adult children to make the transition into being parents and building bounce with their own children.

When it comes to building bounce with our adult children, it is important to remember that we are no longer the primary problem solvers in their lives. Instead of solving problems, we are joining them in their problem-solving process. At the adult stage, the parent no longer tries to fix the problem; rather, the parent joins in without fixing or minimizing the problems being faced. We want our kids to know they are not alone in their problems, that we are happy to play the role of sounding board as they think through problems and scenarios. Just as we would use VCR with our spouse during times of distress and difficulty, we similarly use the VCR process with our adult children.

It is normal for a parent to feel a certain degree of helplessness, even hopelessness about a hard situation their child is dealing with. But the key is not fixing the problem or minimizing the child's emotions; rather, it is to empower the child to navigate this in a satisfying manner.

CORRECTING OUR ADULT KIDS WITH CARE

Correcting adult kids is a significantly different process than correcting children. At the child stage we are still clearly in the mode of "I'm the authority and you need to obey." At the adult stage, we deal with correction as one adult to another. For example, if my child was renting an apartment from another adult, there would be rules and consequences related to that relationship. In the same way, if my adult child is living in my home, we need to agree on what the rules are going to be and what the consequences are if they are not followed. When there is high trust in the relationship, you don't need many rules. When trust has been violated repeatedly, the need for clearly defined rules and consequences increases.

Sometimes we rescue our kids for our own benefit rather than theirs.

Here are a few dos and don'ts to keep in mind when it comes to correcting adult children with care.

• **Don't** *minimize your adult child's problems.* We minimize problems when we don't want to be bothered by the hassle of parenting or when we don't take the time to understand how big our kids' emotions are.

• **Don't** *rescue your adult child from failure.* Leave space to learn from failure. If you rescue your child from a bad grade by jumping in at the last minute to fix their projects or their homework, you aren't doing them any favors. If they can't pay their rent, you can problem solve with them, but if you rescue them (pay the rent without it being attached to a plan), you aren't helping them deal with life as an adult.

Sometimes we rescue our kids for our own benefit rather than theirs. We don't want to face the emotions it will create for us, or the consequences we will have to navigate. In the end, however, it is better for young adults to experience failure early in life while the consequences are less permanent and let them learn from their mistakes while they are young and the stakes are lower.

- **Do *practice mutual problem-solving*.** Parents can help their adult children solve problems, but the problem-solving needs to be part of a mutually agreed upon plan. For example, one of my adult kids is in college, the other in grad school. My wife and I sat down with each of them separately to put a plan on paper about how much debt they were willing to take on, what we could do to help, and what they were going to need to take on as their part. Both of them had enough adult skills that they actually had plans already put together and took responsibility for the process. They knew what kind of help they needed and asked for it.

Parents often have a role to play in solving problems for their adult kids, but we need to avoid the temptation to make things easy on ourselves by taking over and solving problems for them. It can be painful to watch our kids make foolish decisions we know are going to end badly. It can be really easy to want to make that pain go away (for them and for us) by rescuing our adult kids.

It is especially painful when they cut us off from the process of helping. Some of the deepest pain I have seen parents of adult kids go through are those times when the kids reject the parents' worldview, values, and ultimately the relationship itself. You can't always fix those kinds of problems. Sometimes you just have to go through the storm. In seasons like these, we need to look to our own emotional resilience and prepare to open the door to relationship in the future as changes come.

- **Do *follow through on consequences.*** We see the need for consequences most clearly with parents whose adult children have fallen into addiction. Addiction is an indication some—or many—of the infant and child skills were never mastered.[8] Navigating this terrain is not easy. All too often, it is easy to enable our children and keep them from experiencing the consequences of their actions. However, in most cases, this simply prolongs the inevitable crash and can sometimes make it harder later. Fear and guilt are often the motivating forces behind parents who enable their children, which stunts their growth.

- **Do *build a relational bridge*.** We always want to build a clear path to relationship with our adult kids, even if we have had to let them feel consequences. They need to know we want them in our lives and that we love them even when we disagree or even if we are refusing to rescue them. They need to know there is a path to restoration and that you want the relationship.

DEVELOP DISCIPLINES RELATIONALLY WITH ADULTS

At the child stage, the focus is on building personal disciplines. This will continue throughout life. We want to be the sort of people who keep growing our skills and mastering new disciplines for as long as we live. I often think of Benjamin Franklin who reportedly taught himself to play the violin at age seventy. However, at the adult stage there is a new focus when it comes to disciplines. Instead of simply focusing on what is satisfying to us, we begin to focus on what is mutually satisfying to our people. Group projects become important. The ability to get work done collaboratively and not simply in isolation is part of the adult skill set.

One of the ways we can help with this as parents is by working on projects together. Once my son became a teenager, I (Marcus) rarely fixed anything around the house without including him. I wanted him to have as much experience as he could get before moving out on his own. He is actually more intuitive with mechanical devices than I am, and I often seek his input on interpreting installation instructions (since I seem to assemble items backwards the first time I try!). When my daughter's car needed a new headlight, we worked on it together, and now she has that skill, and we have that shared memory.

One of the roles I (Marcus) play now is that of cheerleader. I am available to mentor and coach, but more and more I express pride and offer encouragement as my adult kids continue to grow their skills and learn new disciplines.

THE PATH AHEAD

Parenting joy-filled adults is all about support, encouragement, and guidance while avoiding the classic error of trying to fix problems for them. A number of changes arise during puberty, which add complexity to starting this new stage of growth. We can help our children adjust to the new stage with a rite of passage along with some steps to acknowledge this transition. Developing a group identity is a foundational task for adults; this means bonding with peers provides more opportunities for joy. Mentors add momentum to this process of growth. Demonstrating how to use power for good becomes crucial for our children to learn that true power protects, nourishes, and cares for others. This new stage of life is filled with opportunities for growth for both parents and their children. Fear has no place in this new adventure.

HABIT BUILDER #11—*Lassoing fears*

We all have fears about launching our kids into the adult world. What fears come up as you think about your child transitioning into the adult stage of life?

When our fear stays undetected, we can end up enabling our adult children, which stunts their growth. Parents can go to extremes in this regard. Some will adopt a "hands-off" approach and leave children to figure everything out on their own. Others prefer a "hands-on" approach where they control and smother their child, which restricts joyful growth. Can you relate to one extreme over the other?

One of the most common fears we face as parents is the fear of failing to protect our children from danger. What do you feel the need to protect your adult child from? What is healthy and what is unhealthy in your thoughts and feelings? This can be a good time to talk with friends and other parents about your thoughts and struggles for some perspective and wisdom from those "who have been there before."

HABIT BUILDER #12—*Legacy and life lessons*

The transition of our children into the adult stage of life provides a good opportunity to review the lessons you always wanted to be sure you pass on to your child as part of your legacy.

1. What wisdom or life lessons did your parents teach you? Are there any you want to pass on?
2. What are some essentials you have learned that you want your child to know now that adulthood has arrived? Make a list.
3. Consider a meaningful way you can express your love and joy to your child as an acknowledgment your child is entering adulthood. Find a creative way (letter, gifts, experiences) to convey your love and your dreams for your young adult.

- Include the heart qualities you see in your child that make you smile.
- Include the behaviors you see in your child that make you proud.
- Include the life lessons you want your child to learn from you.

In chapter 4, Marcus shared how he and his wife, Brenda, gave their son a framed family crest, along with a Roman sword to hang in his room as a reminder about his family legacy. Consider a meaningful act or some special gift you can give your adult child to honor him or her in this new stage of growth. This is the reminder about who they are meant to be. As part of this gift you can share a story, review family pictures, and come up with creative ideas to share your gift as a "big picture" reminder your child can receive from you.

CHAPTER 6

The Oxygen Mask

CHRIS AND I (MARCUS) have flown on a lot of airplanes. In all likelihood, you have as well. On every flight the attendants stand in the aisle and explain the safety instructions, including demonstrating use of the oxygen mask. The attendants usually say something like this:

> In the event of a decompression, an oxygen mask will automatically appear in front of you. To start the flow of oxygen, pull the mask toward you. Place it firmly over your nose and mouth, secure the elastic band behind your head, and breathe normally. Although the bag does not inflate, oxygen is flowing to the mask. If you are travelling with a child or someone who requires assistance, **secure your mask on first, and then assist the other person**. Keep your mask on until a uniformed crew member advises you to remove it.[1]

The line we want to emphasize is the one in bold: "secure your mask first, and then assist the other person." This is good advice. Not only is it appropriate when it comes to oxygen masks and airplanes, it is crucial when it comes to joy and parenting.

If we are going to raise joy-filled kids, we need to develop the habit of building our own joy. If we run on low joy for too long as parents, we get grumpy, more easily triggered, and find it harder to regulate our emotions well. Growing our own joy levels is an important part of raising joy-filled kids.

USE YOUR JOY SWITCH TO STAY RELATIONAL

As we mentioned earlier, the Joy Switch in your brain controls your ability to be present and engaged. You cannot be your best self unless your relational circuits are on and running properly. When they are on, your relational self is free to engage creatively with the people around you. However, when they are off, you lose access to the part of your brain that remembers who you are. As a result, you stop acting like yourself. You get upset more easily. You snap at others more quickly or may even shut down and disappear completely.

Sometimes the relational circuits do not fully turn off, but they dim. We don't completely shut down, but we feel like we are barely hanging on. When we are tired, overwhelmed, frustrated, or preoccupied we are unable to fully engage with our children. This is why it is so important to put on our oxygen mask by keeping our own joy levels replenished.

In our book, *The 4 Habits of Joy-Filled Marriages*[2] we identify key practices for keeping joy levels in our marriages high. The same habits apply to the task of keeping joy levels high as we parent. The rest of the chapter will explore what this looks like. We all know that parenting (and life in general) can suck the joy out of us now and then. Building habits that help us replenish our joy levels can be a game-changer for parents.

PLAY TOGETHER

Playing is a great way to grow relational joy. Whether it is playing with our kids, playing with our spouse, or playing with friends, we all need a certain amount of play in our lives to maintain and grow our capacity for joy. In his book, *Play: How It Shapes the Brain, Opens the Imagination, and Invigorates the Soul*, Dr. Stuart Brown writes, "I have found that remembering what play is all about and making it part of our daily lives are probably the most important factors in being a fulfilled human being."[3]

We play with our babies every time we do a joy workout. Simple games like peekaboo and making funny faces and sounds at each other can build joy. Taking breaks and finding time for rest on baby's schedule makes these workouts complete and satisfying for both infant and parent.

When we play with our children, we grow their imagination, their skills, and their sense of joy that we are their parents. Most kids love wrestling games. I (Chris) love roughhousing with my boys. Their energy levels go through the roof and they always finish with lots of joy and satisfaction from the rough and tumble time. Occasionally, they even move the furniture and turn the living room into a WWE arena. This is also true with girls. My (Marcus's) daughter was asked while she was in kindergarten what her favorite activity was, and she said, "I like it when my dad beats me up." I wasn't too excited about her wording, but she meant that she loved it when we play-wrestled. Other ideas:

Creating worlds together. Legos, Lincoln Logs, building tents with blankets, or pretending to be superheroes or adventurers from the past can fire the imagination and help us bond over play. Writing and telling stories is a natural outflow of this. I (Marcus) used to tell both of my kids stories at bedtime. I called them, "To Be Continued" stories so I could quit when I grew too tired, but to this day they smile and relive those moments of joy when they think about "To Be Continued" stories.

Doing crafts together. Painting, drawing, constructing toys, assembling models, doing puzzles—all of these sorts of activities are great ways to bond and give you something to celebrate with a feeling of relational joy and satisfaction.

Learning skills together. You can turn chores into games, you can teach skills and celebrate the victories. Our (Chris and Jen's) boys learned how to knit and sew at school. It was hard at first. It wasn't easy to tie off the knots. The goal was to let the kids struggle through to a successful outcome, even if the struggle was hard. Parents were encouraged to be with the kids, coach and encourage them, but avoid doing the steps for them. By being relational as the child worked hard, it taught the kids the value of working for and waiting for something satisfying.

Here are a few other ideas for building joy through relational skill development.

- Fishing
- Camping
- Biking
- Lawn care
- Cooking/baking
- Field trips. Taking our kids berry picking, apple picking, visiting farms, libraries, monuments, and museums.
- Sports
- Music
- Art

Besides playing with our kids, taking time to play together as husband and wife is really important. We need to keep the joy levels replenished in our marriage or it can sabotage our capacity to parent well.[4]

LISTEN FOR EMOTIONS

If our goal is to maintain our own joy levels, and joy is relational, then one of the more important habits to cultivate is learning to listen for emotions and not just problems. This applies in all of our relationships, but especially with our kids and our spouses. Attuning to our kids' emotions involves learning to listen for their emotions and not just their problems. Many of us are well practiced, left-brain listeners. That means we listen for our kids' problems and are quick to solve them, but we often skip the important step of attuning first by listening for the emotions involved. This is a much more right brain–oriented task. It requires us to read body language and listen for verbal cues that our kids are overwhelmed in some way and need to be seen and feel understood.

The primary goal of listening for emotions is that people feel connected rather than alone. Feeling like you are not alone in a problem makes it more manageable. As parents, the more often we can encourage each other by listening for each other's emotions and not simply fixing each other's problems, the more capacity we will have for the parenting journey.

APPRECIATE DAILY

Our point of emphasis here is not just showing appreciation to our kids. That is important too. But we bring it up in this context as a way of keeping our own joy levels high. Appreciation is packaged joy. It is remembering, feeling, and sharing joy. Taking time to remember joyful memories and letting ourselves relive those experiences so that we feel the joy again is good for our bodies and good for our hearts. Joy grows more when we share it with others and they enter in and enjoy the benefits. This is one of the great things about joy—you don't lose it when others share it. Joy continues to grow.

As I (Marcus) write this, I remember a moment when I played in a camp softball game. I was well into my fifties and well past my prime (I probably shouldn't have even been playing). But my family was there, including my teenage son who had never seen me play before. I felt like I did when I was in Little League and I saw my dad show up to watch the end of the game. I wanted my son to see me play well.

It was a dramatic moment. The bases were loaded with two outs in the last inning and our team was losing by two runs. Suddenly I had one of those moments where everything slowed down and all the old muscle memory from years of baseball as a kid and a teenager came back. The pitch was a little outside, so I went with it and hit a line drive into the gap that rolled into a cornfield and

It is a great idea to have a list of favorite stories that make you feel joy when you go back and relive them.

ended the game with a grand slam. I smile even now as I write this, remembering how it made me feel and how much joy I felt not just from the accomplishment but from the chance to share the moment with my family. The joy grew as more and more people shared the moment with us.

Taking five minutes a few times a day to relive moments like this and let your body feel the energy is a great way to anchor your life in joy. In fact it is a great idea to have a top ten list of favorite stories that make you feel joy when you go back and relive them. You might want to take a few minutes to make a list of happy memories, then give each one a title, and begin collecting pictures and souvenirs that remind you of them. For example, if you loved the lake as a kid, maybe find an old photo of a day at the lake and mount it on a wall in your home.

Keeping our appreciation levels high gives us the strength to navigate the hard stuff. You can't control whether people appreciate you and share that appreciation with you, especially not your kids. This is one of the reasons it is important to remind yourself regularly what you do enjoy. Making this a daily habit can go a long way toward helping you replenish your joy.

Telling appreciation stories to your family is a great

way to keep happy memories alive and build a legacy of joy in your family. My wife, Brenda, tells stories over and over again about happy memories during the weeks spent at her grandparents' house, including family vacations to national parks around the country and special moments from when our kids were young. They have become part of the larger story in which we all live. Often, once someone starts sharing a joyful memory, it triggers someone else to tell a story of joy. My kids might tell stories from their own moments in sports, or special times with friends at the lake, or theater productions they have been in. Before you know it, everyone is smiling and happy to be together as we share each others' joy in the memories that are sweetest to us.

NURTURE A RHYTHM

The goal of the PLAN habits listed here is to help you grow your ability to live life with joy and do it for a long time. In order to sustain our ability to parent well for decades, we need to establish habits that keep our own joy levels high. One of the most important habits we can develop is nurturing a rhythm. Here are some examples of what this might look like.

1. Establish a bedtime routine. Bedtime is for helping everyone calm down and quiet. This time is for helping everyone know that we are happy to be together and that no one is alone even if they are in their own room. It is hard to overstate how important it is to end your day with the sense that you are not alone in this world—that you have people who are for you and love you regardless of what happens.

At the infant level, the bedtime routine in my (Marcus's) home was often a dark room, a rocking chair, a bottle, and singing softly. With our kids, the bedtime routine started with them getting themselves ready for bed, then stories, prayers, and often back rubs before we said goodnight. As adults it is not uncommon to have a quick text or phone call to catch up on the day or share a funny meme several times a week. Our adult kids have their own routines for quieting, but it is nice when they include us from time to time.

> *It is hard to overstate how important it is to end your day with the sense that you are not alone in this world.*

As husband and wife, we have our own routines. One of them is to finish talking about all of the problems in the world or in our family or the workplace before we go to bed. We don't want the bedroom to become the boardroom. We want it to be a happy, peaceful place.

2. Establish a morning routine. When our (Marcus and Brenda's) kids were in school, morning routines had to be quick. There was a lot to get done. We tried to have special breakfasts a couple times a week with pancakes and eggs and the like. Dad was nicknamed "breakfast man" for a while. We also tried to be sure they left for school with a positive experience whenever possible. When we (Chris and Jen) drive our sons to school, we like to practice appreciation and gratitude on the way, to be sure our boys' joy tanks are full before class begins.

I (Marcus) grew up in a family that started the morning with my dad reading from a devotional book and praying for us. I don't remember many of those devotionals, and I remember wishing we didn't have to sit through them sometimes, but as I look back on it now, I appreciate the anchor it gave to each day. With my own kids, we often had "family church" on Sunday. Sometimes we would go to the park and play and have a picnic, then include a time of teaching and praying. At other times, we would build a fire in the fireplace, read the Bible, and pray together before doing fun family things together. Practices like these helped bring a sense of stability and promote an anchor of faith for our family.

3. Build joy before doing hard things. If you know you have to have a hard conversation or tackle a tough situation, it is a good practice to take a few minutes to build some relational joy before you dive in. This "joy charge" is a lot like charging your batteries before you know they are going to get drained. For example, if I need to talk about money with my wife, it is a good idea to schedule a time for it and sandwich the experience around something we both enjoy, like cuddling on the couch, watching a favorite show, grabbing a cup of tea, or sharing positive stories from the week. It is easier to talk about hard things when we are happy to be together than when we start out stressed.

4. Return to joy after doing hard things. One of the tougher parts of parenting can be returning to joy after hard things happen. When you have an argument with your husband or leave a conversation with your kid feeling disrespected and misunderstood or you get bad news from school or the doctor, having a plan for bouncing back is helpful. If we don't have a plan, we will tend to get stuck in our negative emotions and turn to our own addictions for comfort. Here are some simple tactics to try.

- Take a walk.
- Call a friend.
- Write out your emotions and process them in a journal.
- Schedule a time to discuss the issue with your wife or husband. Prepare them for the issue so you can build some joy before you tackle the issue.
- Put together a plan that keeps the relationship bigger than the problem but addresses the problem.

The better we become at bouncing back from hard things, the more capacity we will have for the journey of life.

5. Create a joy calendar. Anticipation is an important element in building joy. When you have something to look forward to it can give you the boost you need to get through the hard stuff. Surprises are nice, too, but having a calendar of relational times you can look forward to is a good practice. It can be as simple as Taco Tuesday or Date Night Thursday, but putting things on the calendar that are relational and fun help create a rhythm for life.

We suggest having weekly, monthly, and quarterly or annual events that you know you can look forward to. I have many good friends who schedule a big trip once a year. Planning the trip allows hours of joy as they anticipate the big event. Sometimes the anticipation is better than the event itself, but it all combines to build joy and nurture a rhythm that makes life sustainable over the long haul.

THE PATH AHEAD

We opened this book with a clear expectation: "By the time you are finished reading this book, we hope you will agree that families exist to grow joy." If we have done our job well, you not only agree with this premise but also feel like you have a clear sense of the path you need to take in your own family.

Parents who don't learn to build joy will default to fear. Fear is the opposite of joy. It is the sense that we are alone with our problems and beyond our capacity.

Fears thrive when joy is neglected. Our goal has been to encourage you with the hope that joy-filled families are possible, and to offer some guidance on how to be intentional about growing joy both in your family and yourself.

We hope you will use the Habit Builders at the end of each chapter to start making some important assessments about your approach to parenting and to start building some crucial skills you will need on this journey. Remember that this is a marathon. Each day is a chance to practice. It is a chance to learn from our mistakes and take a step forward. Improving how well you repair damage in your relationships is just as important as improving the skills that create joy-building habits.

Raising joy-filled kids doesn't mean our children are happy all the time. It certainly doesn't mean that we, or our kids, are perfect. It is about building our own resilience and helping our kids grow theirs. When we succeed in helping our kids grow their emotional capacity, it accomplishes some very profound results.

- Our kids learn they are never alone in this world.
- Our kids develop the skills to make friends wherever they go.
- Our kids learn how to bounce back from hard experiences and eventually be the sort of people who helps others bounce back as well.
- Our kids learn to dream and treat life as an adventure.

- Our kids live with hope—not because the world is getting better and better (when has that ever happened?), but because they know how to find peace and return to joy when bad stuff happens.

Books on parenting can feel like a long list of ways we can mess up. We hope this has not been the case here, but that you have found practical ways to improve or confirm your approach to building joy into kids. After all, that's what families are for.

Acknowledgments

THE IMPETUS for this book was the attachment theory and neuroscience we were introduced to by Dr. Jim Wilder over fifteen years ago. Jim continues to be a good friend, and we are grateful for the work he has done to carve a path for us to follow.

Of course, books like these take a team, and we are very thankful to our wives and families for their input and support. We are also grateful to the team at Northfield, and especially our editors, Duane Sherman and Betsey Newenhuyse.

Notes

CHAPTER 1: WHY IS PARENTING SO HARD?

1. For more about this program visit ThriveToday.org.
2. Daniel J. Siegel, *The Developing Mind: Toward a Neurobiology of Interpersonal Experience* (New York: The Guilford Press, 1999), 67–120.
3. These habits are explained in detail in Marcus Warner and Jim Wilder, *Rare Leadership: 4 Uncommon Habits for Increasing Trust, Joy, and Engagement in the People You Lead* (Chicago: Northfield, 2016).

CHAPTER 2: AS SIMPLE AS ABCD

1. Building Bounce is a registered trademark by Stefanie Hinman and is used here with permission. For more information, see Stefanie's website, healingexpressionskc.com; and Marcus Warner and Stefanie Hinman, *Building Bounce: How to Grow Emotional Resilience* (Carmel, IN: Deeper Walk, 2020).
2. Stuart Brown with Christopher Vaughan, *Play: How It Shapes the Brain, Opens the Imagination, and Invigorates the Soul* (New York: The Penguin Group, 2009), 82.
3. For more on this see Milan and Kay Yerkovich, *How We Love: Discover Your Love Style, Enhance Your Marriage* (New York: WaterBrook, 2017), 12–24.

4. Learn more with Chris M. Coursey, *Transforming Fellowship: 19 Brain Skills That Build Joyful Community* (Coursey Creations, LLC, 2016) and the allegorical book by Denesia Christine Huttula, *The Bridges of Chara: An Allegory of Your Brain's Emotional Landscape* (self-pub. 2015).

5. E. James Wilder, *The Complete Guide to Living With Men* (Pasadena, CA: Shepherd's House, Inc., 2004), 285–99.

CHAPTER 3: RAISING JOY-FILLED INFANTS

1. The vast writings and books by Dr. Allan Schore (allanschore.com) discuss this brain system, while Dr. Jim Wilder (lifemodelworks .org) applies this research to relationships.

2. Ibid.

3. Learn more with E. James Wilder, Edward M. Khouri, Chris M. Coursey, Shelia D. Sutton, *Joy Starts Here: The Transformation Zone* (East Peoria, IL: Shepherd's House, Inc., 2013).

4. The right orbital prefrontal cortex is the part of the brain that thinks of itself as "me." It is located just behind the right eye. It is present at birth, has important growth spurts early in life, and does not finish developing until the early twenties.

5. E. James Wilder, *The Complete Guide to Living With Men* (Pasadena, CA: Shepherd's House, Inc., 2004), 285–99, 38–39.

6. Based on the work and writings of Dr. Jim Wilder, captured in Barbara Moon, *Handbook to Joy-Filled Parenting* (self-pub. 2007).

7. Taken from the Thrive-at-Home teachings (thrivetoday.org) by Dr. Jim Wilder based on the research of Dr. Allan N. Schore (allanschore .com).

8. Learn more about the visual-facial attachment communication in the work of Dr. Allan Schore (allanschore.com).

9. A dyadic relationship is a technical term for a relationship between two people, as opposed to three or more. Allan N. Schore, *The Development of the Unconscious Mind* (New York: W. W. Norton & Company, 2019), 35.

10. Trauma can be defined as anything that causes damage to the development process. Everyone experiences some trauma. Part of the process of maturing is learning how to recognize and rebuild areas of development that have been stunted by trauma.

11. Catherine E. Laing, "Here's Why 'Baby Talk' Is Good for Your Baby," The Conversation, November 10, 2016, https://theconversation.com/heres-why-baby-talk-is-good-for-your-baby-68216.

12. Schore, *The Development of the Unconscious Mind*, 36.

13. Deb Dana, *The Pocket Guide to the Polyvagal Theory: The Transformative Power of Feeling Safe* (New York: W. W. Norton & Company, 2017).

14. Schore, *The Development of the Unconscious Mind*, 37.

15. Learn more about Skills 9 and 15 that keep play safe in Chris M. Coursey, *Transforming Fellowship: 19 Brain Skills That Build Joyful Community* (Coursey Creations, LLC, 2016).

16. Marcus Warner and E. James Wilder, *Rare Leadership: 4 Uncommon Habits for Increasing Trust, Joy, and Engagement in the People You Lead* (Chicago: Northfield, 2016); see also Marcus Warner and Chris Coursey, *The 4 Habits of Joy-Filled Marriages: How 15 Minutes a Day Will Help You Stay in Love* (Chicago: Northfield, 2019).

17. Taken from the Thrive-at-Home teachings (thrivetoday.org) by Dr. Jim Wilder, based on the research of Dr. Allan N. Schore (allanschore.com).

18. Learn more with the writings of Dr. Jim Wilder at lifemodelworks.org.

19. Wilder, *The Complete Guide to Living with Men*, 29.

20. Ibid., 30.

21. Allan Schore identifies shame as a primarily right-brain emotion that does not become toxic until the left brain gives it meaning.

22. This concept is explained in greater detail in the insightful book by E. James Wilder, *The Pandora Problem: Dealing with Narcissism in Our Leaders and Ourselves* (Carmel, IN: Deeper Walk, 2019).

CHAPTER 4: RAISING JOY-FILLED CHILDREN

1. Marcus Warner and Stefanie Hinman, *Building Bounce: How to Grow Emotional Resilience* (Carmel, IN: Deeper Walk, 2020), 31–33.

2. See Chris Coursey, *The Joy Switch: How Your Brain's Secret Circuit Affects Your Relationships—and How You Can Activate It* (Chicago: Northfield, 2021); see also Marcus Warner and Chris Coursey, *The 4 Habits of Joy-Filled Marriages: How 15 Minutes a Day Will Help You Stay in Love* (Chicago: Northfield, 2018) for more about relational brain circuits and the switch in the brain.

3. A similar process is described as an envelope conversation in Marcus Warner and E. James Wilder, *Rare Leadership: 4 Uncommon Habits for Increasing Trust, Joy, and Engagement in the People You Lead* (Chicago: Northfield, 2016), 133–134. Marcus Warner and Chris Coursey, *The 4 Habits of Joy-Filled Marriages: How 15 Minutes a Day Will Help You Stay in Love* (Chicago: Northfield, 2019) and relational sandwiches in E. James Wilder, Edward M. Khouri, Chris. M. Coursey, Shelia D. Sutton, *Joy Starts Here: The Transformation Zone* (East Peoria, IL: Shepherd's House, Inc., 2013).

4. E. James Wilder, *The Complete Guide to Living with Men* (Pasadena, CA: Shepherd's House, Inc., 2004), 60. Trying to train children under age five to hard things will only discourage them because their brain has not yet developed that capacity.

5. The parent's ability to tell a coherent life story is one of the best predictors of how securely attached the child is to the parent. Dr. Cynthia Levin, "Interview with Daniel Siegel, MD," MentalHelp .net, An American Addiction Centers Resource, https://www.mentalhelp.net/blogs/interview-with-daniel-siegel-md/.

CHAPTER 5: JOY-FILLED ADULTS

1. Stuart Brown with Christopher Vaughan, *Play: How It Shapes the Brain, Opens the Imagination, and Invigorates the Soul* (New York: The Penguin Group, 2009), 109.

2. "Brain Development: Teenagers" Raising Children Network, last updated January 7, 2020, https://raisingchildren.net.au/pre-teens/development/understanding-your-pre-teen/brain-development-teens.

3. Microaggressions are words or statements that communicate dismissal or disdain for a person based on their group identity. People often don't realize their words have this effect, but they are offensive and hurtful to those who receive them. Thus, the words have an aggressive, attacking effect on the hearer.

4. Learn more about a rite of passage with E. James Wilder, *Just Between Father and Son: A Weekend Adventure Prepares a Boy for Adolescence* (Downers Grove, IL: InterVarsity Press, 1990).

5. E. James Wilder, *The Complete Guide to Living with Men* (Pasadena, CA: Shepherd's House, Inc., 2004), 101-14.

6. Learn more with E. James Wilder, Ed Khouri, Chris. M. Coursey, Shelia D. Sutton, *Joy Starts Here: The Transformation Zone* (East Peoria, IL: Shepherd's House, Inc., 2013).

7. Learn more about heart characteristics in Chris M. Coursey, *Transforming Fellowship: 19 Brain Skills That Build Joyful Community* (Coursey Creations, LLC, 2016) and Amy Brown and Chris Coursey, *Relational Skills in the Bible: A Bible Study Focused on Relationships* (Carmel, IN: Deeper Walk, 2019).

8. To see a list of nineteen skills every adult needs to master, and to learn how to get training in developing these skills, go to Chris Coursey's website: ThriveToday.org. For information on how to help people with addictions see Marcus Warner's book *Slaying the Monster: Six Strategies for Overcoming Pornography* (Carmel, IN: Deeper Walk, 2017).

CHAPTER 6: THE OXYGEN MASK

1. Ashley Halsey III, "Flying and That Oxygen Mask: Here's the Correct Way to Use It," *Washington Post*, April 18, 2018, https://www .washingtonpost.com/news/dr-gridlock/wp/2018/04/18/flying- and-that-oxygen-mask-heres-the-correct-way-to-use-it/. Emphasis added.

2. Marcus Warner and Chris Coursey, *The 4 Habits of Joy-Filled Marriages: How 15 Minutes a Day Will Help You Stay in Love* (Chicago: Northfield, 2019).

3. Stuart Brown and Christopher Vaughan, *Play: How It Shapes the Brain, Opens the Imagination, and Invigorates the Soul* (New York: The Penguin Group, 2009), 6.

4. For ideas and exercises you can do to build joy in your marriage, see our book *The 4 Habits of Joy-Filled Marriages: How 15 Minutes a Day Will Help You Stay in Love.*

About the Authors

DR. MARCUS WARNER is the coauthor of books like *Rare Leadership in the Workplace* and *The 4 Habits of Joy-Filled Marriages*. He lives with his wife, Brenda, near Indianapolis, Indiana, and has two grown children. Dr. Warner provides training in corporate and nonprofit settings and serves as president of the Christian nonprofit Deeper Walk International. He is passionate about helping people win life's battles and live with greater relational joy.

CHRIS M. COURSEY is a professional trainer, skills coach, author, and international speaker. Chris is the author of *The Joy Switch* and coauthor of *The 4 Habits of Joy-Filled Marriages*. Chris and his wife, Jen, design and lead the THRIVE Training program that uses brain-based exercises to train leaders and families in what experts have identified as the most important relational skills. They are passionate about helping people acquire those skills to make relationships work. Chris and Jen have two sons, Matthew and Andrew.

WHAT SEPARATES HAPPY MARRIAGES FROM MISERABLE ONES?

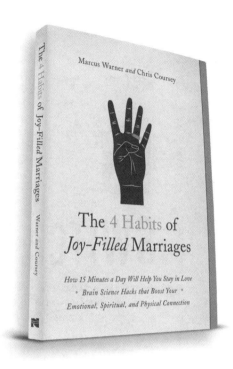

NORTHFIELD
PUBLISHING

These authors have studied relationships (and neuroscience) and discovered four habits that keep joy regular and problems small. Some couples do them naturally, but anyone can learn. Retrain your brain to make joy your default setting by practicing the field-tested 15-minute exercises at the end of each chapter.

978-0-8024-1907-1 | also available as eBook and audiobook

REVIVE YOUR LEADERSHIP.
GROW HEALTHY TEAMS.
SEE GREAT RESULTS.